T0194934

THE Way TO THE MASTER'S HEART

What the Bible Says About Pleasing God

— Ann Perry —

WESTBOW
PRESS®
A DIVISION OF THOMAS NELSON
& ZONDERVAN

All scriptures are from the KING JAMES VERSION (KJV): KING JAMES VERSION, public domain

WestBow Press books may be ordered through booksellers or by contacting:

WestBow Press
A Division of Thomas Nelson & Zondervan
1663 Liberty Drive
Bloomington, IN 47403
www.westbowpress.com
1 (866) 928-1240

ISBN: 978-1-9736-1148-6 (sc)
ISBN: 978-1-9736-1149-3 (hc)
ISBN: 978-1-9736-1147-9 (e)

Library of Congress Control Number: 2017919382

Print information available on the last page.

WestBow Press rev. date: 04/18/2018

DEDICATED TO:

GOD
My Heavenly Father

CZAR PERRY, JR.
My Wonderful Husband

SHAWNDA, BILL, AND MONTÉ
My devoted children

The Way to the Master's Heart
What the Bible Says about Pleasing God

Ann Perry

Thou art worthy, O Lord, to receive glory and honor and power; for thou hast created all things, and for thy pleasure they are and were created.

—Revelation 4:11

CONTENTS

ACKNOWLEDGMENTS

I am grateful to God for trusting me to write such a book about Him. The honor leaves me humbled and excited. I pray that every word will bring Him the glory and honor that He so deserves. He alone knows my earnest desire to joyfully please Him.

Thanks to my *wonderful* husband, Czar Perry Jr., who lovingly supports me in everything I attempt to do for the Lord. I love my husband dearly.

I am appreciative to Ricky Walter and Dorothy Walter who saw this book forming in me before I did. They have been such inspirations! May God continue to use you both to bless the body of Christ with your wisdom, love, and compassion.

I thank the Lord for Sheila Johnson who was such a great encourager during this long process. Blessings to you!

INTRODUCTION

In recent years, my constant prayer has been, "Lord, I want to please You. Teach me how to please You." I finally heard a response, conveyed through the Spirit: He has already told me how to please Him. Those instructions have been divinely preserved and neatly tucked into a book called the Bible. They have not been amended or changed in any way. The Bible is the Word of God! I no longer had an excuse for not knowing how to please Him. That was a breakthrough moment for me!

I had no desire to write a book. There are many inspirational and informative books on the market today. The thought that I might someday write a daily devotional was in the back of my mind, but that was as far as I would go. Nonetheless, when the Holy Spirit spoke to my heart and told me to write, I acquiesced. I put all of my excuses aside and said, "Yes, Lord."

The title of this book is not meant to suggest that God is a man whose heart we are trying to win; nothing could be further from the truth. His love for us is an established fact. "For God so loved the world, that he gave his only begotten Son, that whosoever believeth in him should not perish, but have everlasting life" (John 3:16). Isn't that wonderful? He demonstrated His love for us by sending His Son to die for us while we were in our most unlovable, unrefined state—deeply entrenched in sin. God's love for His creation was settled at Calvary. Winning His heart is not the issue. Exploring what the Bible says about pleasing Him is the sole purpose for this book.

The information I am sharing with you did not start out as a book concept. It comes from my own personal quest for knowing how to please God. This book is the result of searching the Scriptures off and on for three years trying to see what God has to say about pleasing Him. To my amazement, I learned He has plenty to say! *The Way to the Master's Heart* does not claim to be an all-inclusive guide concerning what it takes to please the Lord. It is my prayer that, through your careful examination of the Scriptures, you will add to what has been presented. I invite you to join me on the journey to pleasing God!

It All Begins with Faith

By faith Enoch was translated that he should not
see death; and was not found, because God had
translated him: for before his translation he had this
testimony, that he pleased God. But without faith,
it is impossible to please him: for he that cometh
to God must believe that he is, and that he is a
rewarder of them that diligently seek him.

—Hebrews 11:5-6

*I*t was the last night of the revival. I had purposely put
off going until then so I would not be expected to
attend more than one time that week. I'd been invited
by my good friends Charles and Gwen Washington, who'd recently
accepted the Lord. They were extremely excited about sharing their
life-changing experience with me. There was only one problem: I
could not see why anyone would be excited about going to church
during the week. That was something you did on Sunday, wasn't
it? At least that's what I thought. The Christmas season was upon

us, and it seemed that people would have better things to do than attend a revival.

They invited me on Tuesday, and I promised that I would make my appearance on Friday. My whole week was ruined. I dreaded going, even though I had never attended a revival. When Friday night finally arrived, I seemed to be moving in slow motion. Everything in me was shouting, "Don't go!" But I'd given my word—I had to go. I didn't want to disappoint my friends. Little did I know what God had planned for me!

Upon arriving at the church, I selected a seat in the very back row. It was close to the door, providing a quick escape for me after the service. Dr. E. L. Battles was conducting the services at Taylor's Memorial Church in Corsicana, Texas, where Pastor F. G. Taylor was pastor. Having been brought up in a different denomination, I was not accustomed to the way the service was carried out; it was quite refreshing. The music was captivating. The people dancing and lifting their hands to the Lord was something to behold. "Hallelujah!" and "Thank you, Jesus!" floated from the lips of many of the saints. Some were playing tambourines and someone played the drums. Finally, Dr. Battles stood up and began to preach. When he finished, he invited those who were not saved to come to the altar. It was time for me to leave. I had fulfilled my obligation—I'd shown up!

Suddenly, before I realized what was happening, my feet betrayed me. They were carrying me toward the altar seemingly without my permission. I was no longer in control of my actions. That long walk to the front seemed but a few steps. I found myself kneeling before the altar, surrendering my life to the One who died for me. That was the beginning of my faith walk: December 19, 1970. I said yes to the Lord! He was so pleased!

The Man Who Pleased God

In the early annals of Bible history, the spotlight is shone on a man who pleased God. He is among the descendants of Adam as recorded in Genesis, chapter 5. All the other descendants of Adam lived long lives seemingly without much purpose. Each descendant is said to have lived so many years, "begat sons and daughters" and they died. Nothing noteworthy is said about any of them until one man rises above the rest. His name is Enoch; he became the father of Methuselah and had other sons and daughters. In sharp contrast to the other men, the Bible says: Enoch walked with God; then he was no more, because God took him away (Genesis 5:21-24). It seems that Enoch had a very personal relationship with God. He lived in constant communion and fellowship with God. Because he lived before the Flood and only a few generations from Adam, it is not known how much Enoch knew about God. This story is so amazing because there was no Bible at this time. There was no written record of how to please God. Enoch lived well before God even gave Moses the Ten Commandments and yet Hebrews 11:5 informs us: "for before his translation he [Enoch] had this testimony, that he pleased God". How did he do it? He walked with God by faith! Hebrews 11:6 delivers this profound truth: "But without faith it is impossible to please him: for he that cometh to God must believe that he is, and that he is a rewarder of them that diligently seek him."

Pleasing God is a matter of putting our faith and confidence in Him. We trust Him to be God in our lives. We walk with Him by faith and not by sight (2 Corinthians 5:7). "Now the just shall live by faith: but if any man draw back, my soul shall have no pleasure in him" (Hebrews 10:38). It is crystal clear that our fellowship with God is not dependent upon other people. No amount of religious activities can substitute for our communion with God. We have to learn to walk with God for ourselves. Talking about God is not the same as walking with God.

Pleasing God is a matter of aligning ourselves with the will of God—not through self-effort but by yielding our entire beings to the Holy Spirit. Because He is God, He knows the mind and will of God and He never contradicts Himself. He will always lead us according to the will of God.

I soon learned that living a Christian life requires far more than just the external actions: attending church, contributing to the offering, and being involved in all sorts of church activities. It also entails more than reading the Bible and praying. Don't get me wrong. Every genuine Christian will do all of these things, but they must not be done apart from having a personal encounter with the God of all creation. Loving the Lord and passionately seeking to please Him in every aspect of our lives is fundamental. If our actions do not stem from this intimate relationship with God, it is all in vain.

I entered into relationship with Him through faith. Faith is the complete confidence of a truth that cannot be demonstrated or proved by the process of logical thought. I was not there when they crowned Jesus with thorns. I was not there when they nailed Him to the cross, and yet I believe what the Bible says. He suffered the pain and agony of the cross so I could experience the new birth. He endured a horrific, shameful death so that I might be set free from sin. I was not there, but I believe He rose from the grave with all power in His hand. I believed!

That night at the revival, my life changed forever. I had a changed purpose, changed direction, changed attitude, and changed behavior. I was a new creature (2 Corinthians 5:17). This lifestyle was totally new to me. My parents had taught me to be a morally good person, but I hadn't had a born-again experience to back it up. A few years before I gave my life to Christ, while I was in college, the Lord tugged at the reins of my heart. He placed me in the dormitory with a Christian girl from east Texas. Her name was Shirley, and she loved the Lord with all her heart. I'd never met anyone like her. She prayed in her room every evening at a certain time. I had not heard anyone pray that way before. The young ladies who gathered in Shirley's room were visibly moved by the Spirit, and they cried out to God. That was a bold thing for a teenager to do for the Lord. Shirley was not embarrassed. Her parents were not Christians, and they had forbidden her from spending all of her free time at church. She had to sneak to church. Can you imagine that? She just loved the Lord.

During those evenings spent in prayer, I could feel the Lord gently drawing me toward Him. I could hear Him pleading with me to surrender. I told Him I would come to Him if I could have a little more time. I was still a teenager, and I believed I had a lot of living to do before I could give my life to God. I made a deal with Him (He overlooked my ignorance): I said once I got married and started a family, I would be ready.

As the time went on, I continued to experience an internal emptiness that I could not explain. No matter what I did, I could not fill the void. I was yearning for the Lord, but I did not know it at the time. I tried, without success, to fill that hole with worldly things. How many of you know that only God can fill that spot? Later on in my *new* life, I named the emptiness I had experienced the "God spot." It is as if He deliberately left that hole in my spirit, making it impossible for anything or anyone else to fill it other than His presence.

Trusting God

Life can proceed over pretty rough terrain sometimes. It is only by the grace of God and our faith in God that we are able to make it through. When we keep our eyes fixed on Him amidst difficult circumstances, tragedies, physical suffering, and other dark times in our lives, He is well pleased and will see us safely through.

Have you ever participated in an exercise where you are asked to fall backward into a stranger's arms, trusting them to catch you? In reality, we do that all the time. We trust people we don't know with our lives, with our finances, with our families, etc. And yet when it comes to God, we tend to have trust issues. In Proverbs 3:5–6, Solomon paints a vivid portrait of the nature of our relationship with God: "Trust in the Lord with all thine heart; and lean not unto thine own understanding. In all thy ways acknowledge him, and he shall direct thy paths." Meditating on this passage of Scripture should bring us to the amazing conclusion that we cannot navigate successfully through life without having faith in God.

When we come to the Lord, putting all our trust and faith in Him is essential. It is the foundation on which we build our Christian experience.

God knows what is best for us. He is the all-wise God. His ways and thoughts are well beyond anything we can ever imagine with our human comprehension. As mere humans, we cannot presume to know which way to go. Our dependence on the Father is never bothersome to Him. The only way to truly know how to proceed on this daily journey is to always consult God. We must trust Him completely and without any reservations. He will always lead us in the way we should go. When it comes to living the life of faith, our minds and our hearts have to submit to God.

Walking by Faith

The journey with God always begins with faith. If we are to please Him, we must *continue* in faith. Scripture says, "For therein is the righteousness of God revealed from faith to faith: as it is written, The just shall live by faith" (Romans 1:17). So how do we do that? By taking God at His Word! We believe what God tells us in His Word and we act accordingly. We trust God to be God in every situation.

Our conscious minds will always try to dictate what route we take and what decisions we make. As humans, we are governed by our physical senses. But when we become new creatures in Christ, we have to learn to allow our regenerated spirits to overrule our tendencies to walk by sight. If you can see it, it's not faith.

All of this was completely foreign to me in the beginning of my journey with God. Living a life of faith was a new concept for me. It was a struggle to operate in faith, trusting God's Word when the circumstances were screaming something altogether different. But my Father did not allow me to be taken captive because of my faltering, fragile faith. He held on to me and wouldn't let go! He saw my heart and came to my rescue. How grateful I am! I owe Him my all.

One experience I had early on in my "new life" is forever etched into my memory. Immediately after giving my life to the Lord, we (I; my husband; and my toddler daughter, Shawnda) moved to a small town in New Jersey. I was a new convert hundreds of miles from home. I had no transportation, and there was not a single church in the area. It was a recipe for disaster had it not been for the grace of God.

I was a fledgling Christian, eager to know more about the Lord. Unaware of enemy tactics, I almost fell prey to the teachings of a certain religious group that had invited me to study with them. They'd left some of their literature for me to read. It sounded good to me. I was excited that someone would take the time to come and share with me. I was hungry for the Word.

The Lord blessed me, and I was able to get a job as a clerk in a neighborhood convenience store. It was a small community— everybody knew everybody. One day a stranger dropped in. When he walked into the store, he immediately focused on the reading material I had laid on the counter. It was the material given to me by the religious group. He questioned me about it. After I shared with him what it was all about, he began to open up the Scriptures to me. He provided such a clear understanding of the Bible and what God's plan was for me as a Christian, right away I realized I had been deceived. I trashed all of that material and clung to the Bible, the Word of God. The strange thing about the whole incident is that I had never seen the man before and never saw him again—and I do not recall him buying anything. In retrospect, I decided he was an angel sent by God to put me on the right path. He was sent by God to teach me to walk by faith and not by sight and that God's holy Word needs no assistance. It is sufficient in itself.

Learning to walk by faith is a growing process. We do not become adept and proficient at it overnight. According to the Bible, our faith grows in proportion to our Word intake: "So then faith cometh by hearing, and hearing by the word of God" (Romans 10:17). That is why it so important to feed daily upon the Word of God. Read the Word of God. Meditate on the Word of God. Study the Word of God, and speak the Word of God. Our spirits are nourished and enriched as we take in the nutrients of the Word.

The Bible is always reliable because it is God's word. It has authority because He is the ultimate authority in the universe. Therefore, when we choose to believe God's Word, we are choosing to believe in the God who stands behind His word.

Walking by faith means that we are living out the Word that we are reading, studying, meditating, and speaking. When we walk by faith, we speak faith-filled words—not words of doubt and fear. We have to pay attention to our words. They are containers; they can carry negative or positive. We can speak life, or we can speak death. We can speak blessing, or we can speak cursing. The Bible says, "Death and life are in the power of the tongue" (Proverbs 18:21).

Even our prayers must be faith filled. Mark 11:24 declares, "Therefore I say unto you, What things soever ye desire, when ye pray, believe that ye receive them, and ye shall have them."

The Enemy of our souls is ever working to move us from our faith stance. When we operate in faith, opposition and resistance will most assuredly come. He will try to manipulate us into walking contrary to what the Word says. He will challenge our every move, planting seeds of doubt and unbelief all along the way. Each day we have before us the reality of our physical senses and the reality of God's Word. We can choose to follow our feelings—or we can choose to walk by faith, believing what God's Word says about us, about our situation, about our future.

Faith Is What Activates God's Power in Our Lives

And a certain woman, which had an issue of blood twelve years, and had suffered many things of many physicians, and had spent all that she had, and was nothing bettered, but rather grew worse, When she had heard of Jesus, came in the press behind, and touched his garment. For she said, if I may touch but his clothes, I shall be whole. And straightway the fountain of her blood was dried up; and she felt in her body that she was healed of that plague ... And he said unto her, Daughter, thy faith hath made thee whole. (Mark 5:25–29, 34)

The money she spent did not prosper her in the area where she needed help. It was her faith that activated God's healing power in her life. Still bleeding and weak, this woman spoke faith-filled words: "If I may but touch his clothes, I know I'll be made whole." She did not say, "I hope this works." She *knew* it would work—there was no doubt in her mind. She had no backup plan. Because of her faith, not only was she healed, but she was made whole. Every aspect of her life was complete; there was nothing missing and nothing broken.

Great things can be accomplished with just a small amount of faith. Matthew 17:20 proclaims, "For verily I say unto you, If ye have faith as a grain of mustard seed, ye shall say unto this mountain, Remove hence to yonder place; and it shall remove; and nothing shall be impossible unto you." The key to bringing the power of God into every situation is faith.

People in the world operate out of fear. The people of God operate in faith. Everything in the kingdom of God is operated by faith. Faith is 100 percent focused on the One in whom we believe—not on ourselves or any other person. Jesus said in Mark 11:22, "Have faith in God."

I wish I could say that my journey with the Lord has stayed on course since day one, but I can't. I have been sidetracked and derailed on numerous occasions; yet God has remained faithful to me. He's looked beyond my foolish choices and my lack of consistency and held on to me.

I had the mistaken notion that my new life in Christ would develop automatically. All I had to do was say yes to the Lord and let Him take it from there. *Wrong!* I have since learned that my participation and cooperation on the way to eternity with God is absolutely necessary.

The Last Word

Believing what the Bible says about God and ultimately trusting Him are the first steps to pleasing Him. Trust and confidence in God are the elements to a successful Christian life. We need faith to become a child of God and to progress on the spiritual journey carved out for us by the Lord. It is no wonder that the apostle Paul said, "For we walk by faith, not by sight" (2 Corinthians 5:7).

CHAPTER 2

Watch That Flesh

So then they that are in the flesh cannot please God.

—Romans 8:8

*I*t's all about pleasing Him! The Scripture is explicit: "So then they that are in the flesh cannot please God." Before becoming a "new creature in Christ," I had the mistaken notion that as long as I attended Sunday morning service (the only weekly service that I knew of at our church), I was free to do whatever I pleased. I honestly thought I had rendered my service to God and that He was well pleased with my efforts. But after becoming a "new creature in Christ," I soon realized that there is more to pleasing God than attending church on Sunday. I had to live my life wholly dedicated to the Lord. He is to be glorified in my body and in my spirit because I belong to Him—not just on Sundays, but twenty-four hours a day, seven days a week.

This brought about an intense internal struggle. A war was going on inside of me that I did not quite understand. I had surrendered my life to the Lord—what was the problem? As a babe in Christ, I was unaware of the triple threat to my salvation: the world, the flesh, and the Devil.

I knew the Devil was my enemy. (Everybody knows that.) Peter clearly warns us, "Be sober, be vigilant; because your adversary the devil, as a roaring lion, walketh about seeking whom he may devour" (1 Peter 5:8). As for the world, I knew that I was not to conform to its standards. Paul made that pretty plain in his letter to the Corinthian church when he said, "Wherefore come out from among them, and be separate, saith the Lord" (2 Corinthians 6:17). But the flesh was another matter altogether! Do not be deceived—the flesh is a powerful enemy! It can be lethal to our regenerated spirit.

I do not mean to suggest that at some point in our Christian journey that the struggle between the flesh and the spirit will somehow end. As long as we are in these human bodies, we will have to contend with the flesh and its ungodly desires. But we can take heart in the knowledge that the victory is always ours in Christ Jesus.

I had to come to the realization that just being saved was not enough to combat the flesh. At the time I had no idea what *flesh* meant in a spiritual sense. A simple definition for *flesh* in this context is the tendency to cater to the old nature, our natural sinful desires. The flesh is that enemy within. It was with me everywhere I went. Paul left it on record in these words: "The Spirit and your desires are enemies of each other. They are always fighting each other and keeping you from doing what you feel you should" (Galatians 5:17 CEV).

Turning my life over to God was merely the first step. My sins were forgiven, and I was on the right track. Being born again happened instantaneously. That was the easy part. But now I had to live it out, step by step. I had to learn to take it moment by moment, day by day. If I attempted to look down the road, it became an overwhelming task. From baby saints to seasoned saints, our prayer should be, "Lord, help me to live for you one day at a time." All we have is now. We cannot alter the past, but we can change our future through what we do in the here and now.

Sometimes the Enemy whispers to new Christians, telling them that they will fail. He tells seasoned saints the same thing. He seeks to undermine us in everything we attempt to do for the Lord. His mission is to steal, kill, and destroy (John 10:10). Cunningly and craftily, he uses every failure or shortcoming to his advantage. He constantly reminds believers of where they came from and how they will not be received by other Christians. He specializes in planting seeds of doubt, fear, and discouragement. Then he sits back and waits for them to take root and spring up. When that happens, the flesh can easily revert back to its old practices. This reminds me of a Cherokee Parable:

Two Wolves

An old Cherokee chief was teaching his grandson about life…
"A fight is going on inside me," he said to the boy.
"It is a terrible fight and it is between two wolves.
One is evil – he is anger, envy, sorrow, regret, greed,
arrogance, self-pity, guilt, resentment, inferiority,
lies, pride, superiority, doubt, and ego.

The other is good – he is joy, peace, love, hope,
serenity, humility, kindness, benevolence, empathy,
generosity, truth, compassion, and faith.

This same fight is going on inside you – and
inside every other person, too."
The grandson thought about it for a minute
and then asked his grandfather,
"Which wolf will win?"
The old chief simply replied,
"The one you feed."

-Author Unknown

Indeed, these are words of wisdom. The more we feed the flesh, the stronger it will become. The more we feed the spirit, the stronger it will become. Paul said if we feed the flesh, we will reap corruption, but if we feed the spirit, we will reap of the Spirit everlasting life (Galatians 6:8). If we desire to have everlasting life with God, our goal and aim should be to consistently feed the spirit.

Scripture gives us the key to keeping the flesh in submission. Paul says if we walk in the Spirit, we won't follow the desires of the flesh (Galatians 5:16). What does that mean? If we consistently choose to obey the Spirit of God and the Word of God in all situations, we won't succumb to ungodly desires. Being tempted is not a sin, but the moment we yield to those desires we have displeased God.

There has never been a case in history where the Spirit of God led someone down the wrong path. He is our official guide sent from heaven and is capable of presenting us faultless before the Father (Jude 24). He is all-powerful, but He never forces His will upon us. He is all-knowing, but He will not force His knowledge upon us. We must be willing participants in our walk with the Lord.

On a daily basis, we are faced with the decision between following the Lord or being led away by our own lusts. Even though the choice may sometimes appear overwhelming, the Lord will empower us to overcome those desires and behave in accordance to His Word. We just have to be willing. When we give Him the go-ahead to be Lord in our lives, we have just served notice to the Enemy that he has to contend with the power of God.

All believers should commit 1 Corinthians 10:13 to memory and let the truth of it settle into their spirits: "There hath no temptation taken you but such as is common to man: but God is faithful, who will not suffer you to be tempted above that ye are able; but will with the temptation also make a way to escape, that ye may be able to bear it."

Our actions are the results of our thoughts. That's why it is so important to be careful what we allow to rest upon our minds. Before an act is committed, it is first a thought. Personally, when a temptation arises, I immediately look for the door that God promised—the way of escape. When we fail in times of tests, trials, and temptations, it is because we did not take advantage of the escape route provided to us by God. Contrary to what some people say and think, we don't just fall into temptations. There is always a way out; God promised it in His Word.

Every Christian must learn that when a temptation presents itself, it is not from God. Scripture explicitly tells us that God does not tempt any person: "Let no man say when he is tempted, 'I am tempted by God'; for God cannot be tempted by evil, nor does He Himself tempt anyone. But each one is tempted when he is drawn away by his own desires and enticed. Then, 'when desire has conceived, it gives birth to sin; and sin, when it is full-grown, brings forth death'" (James 1:13–15 NKJV).

I feel I must insert this word of encouragement. There may be times when we fail miserably. We will completely miss the mark! But please hear what the Lord says to us in His Word. "My little children, these things write I unto you, that ye sin not. And if any man sin, we have an advocate with the Father, Jesus Christ the righteous" (1 John 2:1).

When we sin, Jesus is sitting at the right hand of the Father making intercession for us. He is our representative in heaven. God provides a way back into fellowship: "If we confess our sins, he is faithful and just to forgive us our sins, and to cleanse us from all unrighteousness" (1 John 1:9). He is a loving God, and He is not searching for ways to disqualify us. That is the Enemy's job. Scripture declares that he is the "accuser of the brethren" (Revelation 12:10). Had our God wanted to see us destroyed, He would not have sent His only Son to die for our sins. We were already on death row—but God!

A word of advice: If you fall, don't stay there. Rise from the ashes of defeat and move forward in the strength of the Lord. Do as the apostle Paul says in Philippians 3:13–14: "Brethren, I count not myself to have apprehended: but this one thing I do, forgetting those things which are behind, and reaching forth unto those things which are before, I press toward the mark for the prize of the high calling of God in Christ Jesus."

Let go of past failures. Do not dwell on what has happened. Negative thoughts will interfere with your ability to hear the Holy Spirit. If you can't hear Him, how can He lead you? You cannot have a positive life with a negative mind. Paul told the believers at Philippi, "Finally, brethren, whatsoever things are true, whatsoever things are honest, whatsoever things are just, whatsoever things are pure, whatsoever things are lovely, whatsoever things are of good report; if there be any virtue, and if there be any praise, think on these things" (Philippians 4:8). Our adversary knows that if he can control our thoughts, he can control our actions. If we think on the right things, right actions will follow. We can never go wrong when we meditate on God's Word and apply it to our daily living.

God's Power in God's People

In Luke 4, the Bible says Jesus went into the synagogue on the Sabbath day as was His custom. He stood up to read. The Bible goes on to say the following:

> And there was delivered unto Him the book of the prophet Isaiah.
>
> And when He had opened the book, He found the place where it was written,
>
> The Spirit of the Lord is upon me, because he hath anointed me to preach the gospel to the poor; he hath sent me to heal the brokenhearted, to preach deliverance to the captives, and recovering of sight to the blind, to set at liberty them that are bruised.

16

To preach the acceptable year of the Lord. And He closed the book, and He gave it again to the minister, and sat down. And the eyes of all them that were in the synagogue were fastened on Him. (Luke 4: 17–20)

Jesus said, "The Spirit of the Lord is upon me." This was the beginning of His earthly ministry. He did so by first acknowledging the fact that the Spirit of the Lord was upon Him. Jesus was empowered to serve by the Holy Spirit of God! The Bible clearly tells us in Luke 4:1 that Jesus was full of the Holy Ghost! If Jesus needed the indwelling power of God, certainly we need to have Him operating in our lives at all times.

Before the Lord Jesus Christ ascended back to the Father, He commanded the disciples to wait for the promise of the Father (Acts 1:4–5). That promise was the baptism with the Holy Ghost. Jesus told them they would receive power after the Holy Ghost had come upon them (Acts 1:8).

The disciples had already experienced power in their ministries while Jesus was with them. They had power to cast out devils and to heal all manner of sickness and disease. And yet this was not the indwelling power they were going to need.

Because they didn't have the power on the inside, the disciples failed Jesus. Judas betrayed Him. Peter cut off the ear of the servant of the high priest. When Jesus was arrested, Peter disavowed having any connection to Him. Fear gripped their hearts and they all deserted Him. After the resurrection, Thomas doubted Him.

In order to accomplish the mission that God had assigned to each of them, they needed the indwelling of the Holy Ghost. Without the Spirit residing within, the flesh would rule.

We live in a world filled with darkness. Every Christian must strive continuously to live out the message of the gospel of Christ. The only way we can do this is through the work of the Holy Spirit. It is He who equips us to do and to be all that God desires.

God never meant for His people to resemble the world in any shape, form, or fashion. In the book of Genesis when He lovingly crafted man, God said, "Let us make man in our image, after our likeness" (Genesis 1:26). From the very beginning, everything about us was like Him. Genesis records in the third chapter something quite tragic and devastating to mankind. Sin entered the human race because of Adam's disobedience. After that, man no longer resembled the Father. The entire human race was infected. Subsequently, every person born was disfigured and marred.

Because of Jesus, we can now be admitted into the family of God. All we have to do is believe in Him. It has to be more than an intellectual knowledge. Romans 10:9 says we must believe in the heart. When we believe like that, we are instantly transported out of darkness into the kingdom of God.

It is only after this new birth that we begin taking on the image of Christ, little by little. Second Corinthians 3:18 says we are changed into the image of Christ by the Spirit of the Lord; no self-effort can do it. He doesn't do it from the outside. He must indwell and fill us in order to accomplish this work within.

It is impossible to physically go in more than one direction at a time. It is the same way in the spirit. As believers, the Lord wants us to follow Him. We must abandon our own selfish desires, goals, and ambitions and go where He leads. Life in the Spirit means that I trust the Holy Spirit to do in me what I cannot do myself. It is not a case of trying, but of trusting; not a case of struggling, but of resting in Him. We can't live the life of Christ by sheer willpower. But as we completely give up control of all we tend to hold on to and allow the Holy Spirit to rule in every area of our lives, we are gradually shaped and formed into His image.

Becoming like Christ is not an overnight transition; it's a progressive experience. It is a process that demands consistently choosing to do things God's way instead of our own way. Surrendering control of our lives to the Lord is a liberating experience. It is so empowering when we can say, "Holy Spirit, have your way." Instead of being restricting, it is a powerful, life-changing experience when we can say with resolve, "Not my will, but your will be done!"

Because of the shed blood of Christ, believers everywhere can break free and remain free of any ungodly habits, desires, or wrong thinking patterns. All we have to do is invite the Spirit of God to do His work within us. He is always willing. He will renew us, He will refresh us, and He will reshape us and mold our minds.

As believers and followers of Christ, it is our personal responsibility to trust God, honor Him, and seek to please Him. We can have an incredible future with the Lord if we allow Him to take full control. We were created by God, in His image, for a purpose. When He is ordering our steps, we can have confidence in knowing that we will be led into the way everlasting.

What a relief it is to know that we don't have to do this on our own! We couldn't, even if we tried. Our strength alone is no match for the Enemy of our souls. As we consistently rely upon the Holy Spirit's power and guidance and walk in obedience to the Word of God, we are strengthened.

A good way to check our progress in our walk is to examine our lives in light of the Word. Whenever the flesh is in control, it will manifest itself in ungodly behavior and lifestyles.

> People's desires make them give in to immoral ways, filthy thoughts, and shameful deeds. They worship idols, practice witchcraft, hate others, and are hard to get along with. People become jealous, angry, and selfish. They not only argue and cause trouble, but they are envious. They get drunk, carry on at wild parties, and do other evil things as well. I told you before, and I am telling you again: No one who does these things will share in the blessings of God's kingdom. (Galatians 5:19–21 CEV)

After carefully and prayerfully reading Paul's explanation of how the flesh operates, we must never be content if any signs of the flesh are manifesting themselves in our lives. Tolerating fleshly behavior in any shape, form, or fashion hinders us from pleasing the Lord. Giving in to fleshly desires will always get us in trouble with God. As believers, God has called us away from such behavior.

The book of Hebrews contains several warning passages. It is also tempered with wonderful words of encouragement for the people of God. "Therefore, we ought to give the more earnest heed to the things which we have heard, lest at any time we should let them slip" (Hebrews 2:1). This passage was not intended for only the Jewish Christians of that era but for Christians in general. Hebrews chapter one speaks of the superiority of Christ over angels, which gives His message credibility and authority. We must pay attention to the message of Jesus Christ. If we neglect to obey the Word, we are headed for a tragic downfall.

We are forewarned of the danger of living sloppy and careless Christian lives. Serving God halfheartedly is an offense to Him who is perfect in every attribute. We are called to be imitators of Christ—not just in the obvious things, but also in the finer points of life. Everything Jesus said and did was to please the Father. Christians who really love the Lord strive consistently to please Him through faithful obedience to His Word.

We do not have the luxury of picking and choosing what we will obey and what will be discarded. Our role as Christians does not end at church. We are Christians wherever we go. We represent the King! That is a privilege and an honor that should never be taken lightly. Our daily practice and constant effort should be to emulate Him. As new creatures in Christ, we have a changed purpose, a changed direction, a changed attitude, and changed behavior. God wants us to be meticulous in our day-to-day living. Not only is He watching us, but the world is watching. They need to see what it means to be "holy in all manner of conversation" (1 Peter 1:15). They need to see Jesus living in us. Finally, even when we know no human eye can perceive us, the Lord will be truly pleased if we walk worthy anyway.

In the end, a person who continues to follow the flesh will be excluded from the kingdom of God. It stands to reason that if we want to please God, we must constantly yield to the Holy Spirit. His work in us produces all the right things. "But the fruit of the Spirit is love, joy, peace, longsuffering, gentleness, goodness, faith, meekness, temperance: against such there is no law" (Galatians 5:22–23).

His Victory, Our Example

There is an interesting incident recorded in the gospels of Matthew, Mark, and Luke. They each tell of the encounter Jesus had with the Devil in the wilderness. After concluding forty days and forty nights of fasting, the Devil had the audacity to tempt the Son of God. The wicked one approached Jesus three different times with three different temptations. Each time the Lord put him to flight with the powerful Word of God. We, too, must learn to use that same method.

"For we have not a high priest which cannot be touched with the feeling of our infirmities; but was in all points tempted like as we are, yet without sin" (Hebrews 4:15). For quite some time, this passage of Scripture puzzled me. Jesus was tempted those three times in the wilderness, but why is the Bible saying He was tempted in *all points* like we are? What I failed to understand was He did not undergo every single temptation we experience but rather was tempted in the three areas in which all men are tempted: the lust of the flesh, the lust of the eye, and the pride of life (1 John 2:15–17)—another light-bulb moment for me!

Jesus faced temptation at other times in His ministry as well. In every instance, He demonstrated to the Devil and to all of humanity that we can be victorious over temptations. "Wherefore in all things it behooved him to be made like unto his brethren, that he might be a merciful and faithful high priest in things pertaining to God, to make reconciliation for the sins of the people. For in that he himself hath suffered being tempted, he is able to succor them that are tempted" (Hebrews 2:17–18).

The Last Word

Catering to our flesh will take us places we do not intend to go. Getting back on track can be a long and difficult process. Following the tendencies of the flesh will always get us in a world of trouble because it leads us away from God—and that is a dangerous place to be.

There can be only one ruler on the throne of our hearts. Either the Spirit is in control or the flesh is in control; they do not reign together. Pleasing God is simple. Just follow the Spirit of God, and He will never lead you astray!

CHAPTER 3

Celebrate the Lord

I will praise the name of God with a song, and will magnify him with thanksgiving. This also shall please the Lord better than an ox or bullock that has horns and hoofs.

—Psalm 69:30–31

King David discovered the key to having a vibrant relationship with the living God: he was a worshipper from his heart. What was happening in the kingdom or in his own personal life did not matter, he always found time to praise and magnify the Lord. God delights in our praises, though it adds nothing to His perfection. By the same token, if we do not praise Him, He is not diminished in any way. Whether we praise Him or not, God remains the same! If that is so, why are we admonished to praise the Lord and be thankful to Him? Why does that please the Lord?

Scripture tells us that God inhabits the praises of His people. It is where He dwells (Psalm 22:3). Praise brings us closer to Him.

When I was newly saved, this concept was foreign to me. In those early years, watching the saints praising God so fervently and for so long seemed like a complete waste of time. To me it seemed like a delay of the worship service. One would shout, "Glory!" Another would shout, "Hallelujah!" Then someone would grab what we call a "congregational song" and sing until he or she got tired and then someone else would pick it up. It looked to me like things were all out of order. On the contrary, they were absolutely in order. It is always a good thing and a blessed thing to sing and give praises to God.

I am reminded of two preachers who were stripped of their clothes, shamelessly beaten, and thrown into jail after a deliverance service. At midnight, the voices of Paul and Silas rang loudly throughout the prison. They were not weeping and wailing. They were not complaining and feeling sorry for themselves. They were not wallowing in a state of depression. Beaten and bloodied, they were praying and singing praises to God! They had joined the ranks of the other apostles who were happy because God had counted them worthy to suffer for the sake of Jesus (Acts 5:41).

When their prayers reached the throne of God along with their songs of praise, something dramatic and miraculous happened. The bowels of the earth erupted, causing the foundation of the prison to shake. All the prison doors were opened, and everyone's bands were loosed. No one tried to escape. The jailer realized it was a work of God. As a result, he and his entire household believed in Jesus. Those preachers had not been preoccupied with their particular situation. Their joy had not been extinguished by what happened to them. All of their focus remained on God.

Our praise can affect our surroundings. We can literally change the atmosphere. When we experience those midnight times in our lives, trials, and persecutions, we should count it all joy as the believers in the early church did (James 1:2). The other prisoners heard Paul and Silas singing and praising God instead of complaining, mumbling, and grumbling. We may not be aware of it, but others are watching how we respond to our life's situations. God is certainly watching. Our goal and chief desire should be for Him to be pleased with how we conduct ourselves wherever we are. Whether we are in the pit or the palace, God is worthy of our praise.

The Enemy of our souls knows the importance of praise and thanksgiving. He will always attempt to interrupt our praise with various kinds of distractions. He will use anything to try to cause us to shift the focus back to ourselves. I have learned that meditating on my problems and troubles is a serious and dangerous intrusion into my walk with the Lord. When I find myself doing this, I know it is time to do as the men of God did when they were cast into prison—pray and sing praises to the Lord! That pleases God!

A life of continual praise brings glory to God

Many people operate under the misconception that praise has to be done within the confines of the church. Not so! It is important to understand what true praise really is. Oftentimes we are familiar with what it looks like—how others demonstrate praise—but we miss what it is all about. Merely imitating what others are doing does not produce genuine or authentic praise. Praise is preoccupied with who God is and with what He has done.

We praise Him directly by expressing *to Him*; we can also praise God indirectly by commending Him *to others*. Allow me to share an example of just how powerful praise (even indirect) can be. It was a very beautiful day in Kansas City, Missouri. We were there for a church convention. Having just arrived at the hotel, we were leisurely unpacking our things, looking forward to a great week of service. I had the privilege of having a saintly woman named Bertha Davis for a roommate. Neither of us will ever forget what happened. We were engaged in a pleasant exchange about this and that—you know how it is. Our conversation eventually drifted onto the Lord. We were simply talking about His goodness and all that He meant to us.

Suddenly, it was as if all the oxygen was sucked out of the room. At first we did not know what was happening. Weak attempts to continue our dialogue were soon abandoned. Finally, we gave in to the Spirit and became lost in praise and worship. *His presence filled the room!* How sweet it was! Our indirect praise changed to direct praise. He was in the room, and all of our attention was solely upon Him. I can't say how long it lasted, but the experience is forever burned in our memories and our hearts. When it was over we looked at each other and fell over on the bed laughing with joy, wondering if and when He would do it again. No wonder the psalmist said, "In thy presence is fullness of joy; at thy right hand there are pleasures for evermore" (Psalm 16:11). What a wonderful and enriching experience, one we will always cherish. Praise summons the very Presence of God. It creates an atmosphere for His powerful Presence (Psalm 22:3). Something as simple as praise garnered His attention and brought His presence down to us.

God is worthy to be praised (Revelation 4:11, 2 Samuel 22:4, and Psalm 18:3). There is nothing in us worthy of praise; all that is worthy of praise is of God and from God. We praise God because we were created to praise Him.

"But ye are a chosen generation, a royal priesthood, an holy nation, a peculiar people; that ye should shew forth the praises of him who hath called you out of darkness into his marvellous light" (1 Peter 2:9).

As saints of God, praise should flow from our lives in a most natural way. In fact, it is one of the most natural things we can do! The Bible tells us that praising God is becoming and appropriate for the righteous (Psalm 33:1). When we come together and worship, praise does not end when the music stops or when the benediction is given. Acceptable praise comes from the heart and is not generated by the sound of the music. "By him therefore let us offer the sacrifice of praise to God continually, that is, the fruit of our lips giving thanks to his name" (Hebrews 13:15).

King David is one of my favorite Bible characters. He wrote more about praise than any of the other authors of the Bible. It wasn't because his life was going great all the time. On the contrary, his life was filled with trials and tragedies but he always lifted himself above it by praising the Lord. "I will bless the Lord at all times, His praise shall continually be in my mouth" (Psalm 34:1). Apostle Paul concurred with King David as he encouraged the Philippian believers to "Rejoice in the Lord always, and again I say rejoice" (Philippians 4:4). This speaks of a continual action in our daily lives.

We should praise God when we feel like it, and we should praise God when we don't feel like it. Because we have been born again, our wills are no longer subject to the flesh but to our regenerated spirits. Praise is a conscious decision of our wills; we determine that we will praise God in whatever circumstances or situations we find ourselves. Our emotions cannot determine our praise, or we could be in big trouble sometimes. We really need to set praise in motion—especially when we are experiencing turbulent times. It somehow seems to build and multiply. Whether we are on an emotional high or low, whether we feel God's presence or God seems far away, praise is still fitting because God is always there and He never changes.

Genuine praise is always an expression of the heart. David said, "I will praise thee, O Lord, with my whole heart; I will show forth all thy marvellous works" (Psalm 9:1). God is never pleased with halfhearted devotion and praise. This life of praise is a constant and unchanging attitude of gratitude. It is thankfulness to God that comes straight from the heart. It is not just a bunch of words memorized and used in an attempt to persuade or flatter God into doing something not in His will—that can't be done anyway.

He deserves praise! Our daily lives should be lived out seeking to come to know God in a more personal and real way. The more we come to know Him, the more we will praise Him. The more we praise Him, the more of His presence we will experience. Praise lends itself to vocal and physical expression. God has given us voices, hands, and feet with which to express our praise to Him—even more so, with all of our lives. When it comes to praising God, we must do it with reckless abandon.

What does a life of continual praise look like in day-to-day living? It does not mean that every conversation we have has to be about the Lord; that is virtually impossible to do. A life of continual praise is a mindset; it is an attitude that in spite of any negative or challenging situations we find ourselves in, we can still praise God. We reflect on God's goodness and honor Him in all that we say and do. We recognize that our life's situations do not determine God's worth and value to us. He is always worthy of praise. We internalize what the Word says about our God and allow Him to be our sole focus. As we do so, we'll come into agreement with these words: "From the rising of the sun unto the going down of the same the Lord's name is to be praised' (Psalm 113:3).

The Last Word

Whenever something comes out of your mouth and you recognize that it does not honor God, immediately repent and begin to give God praise. What our lips are saying and what fills our hearts have to match up. We do not want to be like those people who Jesus said honored Him with their lips but their hearts were far from Him (Matthew 15:8).

A life of praise says that I serve the true and living God who deserves all my praise. A life of praise honors the Lord at all costs by lifting up God in all situations. Go ahead—celebrate the Lord.

CHAPTER 4

Obedience is the Key

Hath the Lord as great delight in burnt offerings and sacrifices, as in obeying the voice of the Lord? Behold, to obey is better than sacrifice, and to hearken than the fat of rams.

—1 Samuel 15:22

I was a fairly obedient child; however, I do recall a few instances when my judgment was somewhat impaired, causing me to "forget" what I had been told to do or not to do. I didn't get a lot of whippings, but one in particular will stay with me until my last breath. I was sixteen years old (past the age of corporal punishment, I thought). Our school had a track meet in Waco, Texas, and I was allowed to go there on the bus. I was supposed to return the same way I went (on the bus). What harm would it have done for me to stay until the meet was completely over and ride back in a car with some classmates? It seemed like a logical thing to do, so I did it. Unbeknown to me at the time, my mother was frantically going all over the neighborhood asking my friends where I was. When I finally walked in the door, I was greeted by a flying belt wielded by my 4'11' mother. She made no attempt to aim at any particular part of my anatomy; wherever it landed was just all right. I learned a painful lesson in obedience.

Obedience is defined as compliance, agreement, submission, or conformity. The greatest and hardest lesson to learn in our Christian experience is the lesson of obedience. King Saul, Israel's first king, learned it the hard way. Before Saul was anointed king, Samuel served as judge over Israel. He judged well. But when he was old he appointed his sons as judges over Israel, and they did not follow in their father's footsteps. The people used this as an excuse to request a king to reign over them, as was the custom of all the other nations surrounding them. God instructed Samuel to anoint Saul as their king, though it was not His will for them. God was so gracious that He promised to bless them and their king if they would walk in His ways, if they would be obedient to the Lord. Everything went well in the beginning of Saul's reign. He enjoyed great military successes. But he had a dangerous flaw—a bad habit of doing things his own way.

Samuel, by the direct order of God, commanded Saul to "Smite Amalek, and utterly destroy all that they have, and spare them not; but slay both man and woman, infant and suckling, ox and sheep, camel and ass" (1 Samuel 15:3). The Amalekites were a group of people who lived by attacking other nations and carrying off their wealth and their families. When the Israelites entered the Promised Land, the Amalekites were the first to attack them. They continued their raids on God's chosen people at every opportunity. God gave Saul explicit instructions. There was no room for misunderstanding or for misinterpretation. God said what He meant and He meant what He said! Saul and his men did attack the Amalekites, but they spared the king and kept the best of the spoils. This was not what God had instructed!

When he was confronted by Samuel, Saul said: "Blessed be thou of the Lord; I have performed the commandment of the

Lord" (1 Samuel 15:13). Really? Samuel could both hear and see the evidence of Saul's disobedience. He had partially obeyed—but partial obedience is actually disobedience. Saul reasoned that God would be pleased with his actions if he offered a sacrifice to Him. Truth alert: we cannot do things the wrong way expecting right results. Samuel informed Saul that being obedient to God is more pleasing to Him than offering a sacrifice. He was not saying that God disapproved of sacrifices. But a sacrifice has to be performed out of love and obedience—empty rituals do not please the Lord. Disobedience cost Saul dearly; he was rejected from being king.

We, too, are in danger of losing out with God if we stop wholeheartedly following the Lord. Jesus said, "Not everyone who says to me, 'Lord, Lord,' will enter the kingdom of heaven, but only he who does the will of my Father who is in heaven" (Matthew 7:21 NIV). We have no excuse for not knowing what the Lord requires of us. It has been faithfully recorded in the Bible and preserved down through generations. Either we obey or disobey. The choice is ours.

Walking in obedience to God requires that we trust Him completely. That means we have faith to believe that God knows what is best for our lives. We may not understand, but we trust Him because He is God. Psalm 125:1 says, "They that trust in the Lord shall be as Mount Zion, which cannot be removed, but abideth forever."

Sometimes our spiritual journey is like being on the runaway train theme park ride. During my tenure as the youth leader at my church, we took the children to Six Flags Over Texas. Against my better judgment, I let one of the students in the group talk me into riding the "runaway mine train" with him. It took a lot of coaxing, but he sold me when he said it was a fun but not scary ride. He had withheld some of the details of the ride in order to persuade me to take the challenge. Once I was secured in the seat, the ride took off. *This is not too bad*, I thought. *What had I been afraid of?* The train gradually began to pick up speed, but that was all right with me. In fact, I found it rather exhilarating. All of a sudden the train began jerking violently, going faster and faster. It finally slowed down. I breathed a sigh of relief, thinking the ride was over. How wrong I was! That train started doing some stuff that I cannot even recall—up and down, around, fast, slow. I did not know what to expect! The whole time I was screaming at the top of my lungs. I am certain my desperate cries were heard throughout the entire park! In addition to my yelling and pleading to get off, I was threatening to do bodily harm to the young man who convinced me to ride. He thought it was all worth it. He laughed (at me) during the entire course of the ride! For those who are interested, I did him no harm. I was so glad to be safely on the ground when the ride ended that I joined in and laughed at myself.

Just like that train, I have learned that as we live for God our paths can be unpredictable, scary, unsettling, and everything in between. But one thing is sure: our God is faithful! We can trust Him. According to *Merriam-Webster's Collegiate Dictionary*, the word *trust* means "assured reliance on the character, ability, strength, or truth of someone or something." Throughout the Bible, the Lord our God has proved faithful in all those areas. We can trust Him in even the most difficult circumstances.

One person in particular comes to mind when I think about trusting God: Job. He was a prosperous man who lived an upright life before God. God knew the heart of Job and allowed Satan to attack him. When the Enemy's vicious assault was over, Job had lost everything: his children, his wealth, and his health. Even those he considered friends had turned against him. Job had no idea why he was being mysteriously destroyed. Yet in the midst of such devastation and suffering, we hear him triumphantly declaring, "Though he slay me, yet will I trust him: but I will maintain mine own ways before him" (Job 13:15).

When faced with adversity, our reliance upon God's character, ability, and strength is critical. He is the faithful God who will see us through. Isaiah 46:10 says, "Declaring the end from the beginning, and from ancient times the things that are not yet done, saying, My counsel shall stand, and I will do all my pleasure." He is the all-wise God. He knows all things; nothing escapes His all-seeing eye. He knows each of us, and He has a specific plan for our lives. Our heavenly Father always knows best.

In the twenty-ninth chapter of Jeremiah, the people of God found themselves on the opposite side of victory—defeated, humiliated, and destitute. They were uprooted from their land and taken into captivity by the Babylonians. What a tragic end to God's called-out and beloved people! How could they have fallen so far? Where was their mighty protector who had always fought so valiantly for them? What would their final outcome be?

The Scripture is plain. The loving and all-wise God of Israel had purposely allowed the enemy to overrun and capture His chosen people. Jeremiah, the prophet, sent a letter to them in Babylon. They had been remiss in their relationship with the Almighty, failing to obey the Lord. They knowingly and willingly dishonored Him in every way imaginable. Punishment was inevitable.

Their future seemed dark, but God gave His rebellious children a glimmer of hope. He lovingly said to them, "For I know the thoughts that I think toward you, saith the Lord, thoughts of peace, and not of evil, to give you an expected end" (Jeremiah 29:11).

Living obedient lives requires more than external observation of rules and regulations. Our obedience to God flows from an intimate love relationship with Him. David said something quite profound concerning his experience with God: "I will walk within my house with a perfect heart" (Psalm 101:2). He realized the absolute necessity of being upright within his heart. David knew the value of walking with integrity, even in his own house.

In no uncertain terms, the Bible teaches us to "Keep thy heart with all diligence; for out of it are the issues of life" (Proverbs 4:23). In Scripture, the heart of man is our unseen part. It is the core of who we really are; it is the inner person, our central essence. Everything that we think, say, and do, originates in the heart. When we accept the Lord as our Savior, we receive something very precious and valuable: a new heart—a priceless treasure. It is well worth guarding this gift "with all diligence." Protecting and defending our hearts is our personal responsibility; no one can do it for us!

Because our hearts are under constant attack, it is critical that we monitor everything we let in to them. We must fight to keep out any seeds of bitterness, anger, jealousy, resentment, hatred, strife, pride, and unforgiveness. These things are manifested in wrong attitudes and wrong behavior. Jesus said, "The good man brings good things out of the good stored up in his heart, and the evil man brings evil things out of the evil stored up in his heart" (Luke 6:45 NIV). The things we do, whether good or bad, stem from the condition of our hearts. They are a direct reflection of what lies within.

The surest way to guard your heart is to abide in the Lord and let Him abide in you. Allow the Holy Spirit to search your heart often. Quickly get rid of anything that is not God-like by confessing it and asking for His forgiveness. Daily feed the inner man with the Word of God. Stay in fellowship and communion with Him through prayer.

God sees us from the inside out. Our "outside" world must be a true reflection of our "inside" world. If we publicly demonstrate love, purity, and honesty, it must be a genuine expression of our authentic lives. Who we are in private tells the whole story. True communion with the Lover of our souls requires fully surrendering to Him. We are so in sync with Him that wherever He leads, we will follow! Whatever He commands, we will do!

Doing things our own way does not sound so bad until we view it from God's perspective. *Rebellion* is failing to do what God commands. He puts rebellion in the same category as witchcraft! That's something to think about the next time God gives you an assignment of any sort, whether large or small. If God's instructions are not followed, that act of disobedience puts us in the same category with those who dabble in the occult. We can always trust God. He wants to know that He can trust us.

There is an Old Testament story that has much to teach us about being obedient to God. Jonah was a prophet sent to a foreign country to witness to a nation of heathens. The Assyrians were a fierce race of warriors who would later carry the northern kingdom of Israel away captive. This was not an assignment Jonah relished, and he attempted to run away from it by hopping a freighter and going in the opposite direction. Jonah was eventually tossed overboard and subsequently swallowed by a big fish. After the fish vomited Jonah out on dry land, Jonah rushed to do the will of the Lord. Unfortunately, he was angry and bitter. He had no mercy or compassion for the Assyrians. Jonah knew that God would forgive them if they repented.

Jonah had not completely yielded to God. His mind knew God's truth. He finally obeyed God's orders, but he did not do the will of God from his heart. Ephesians 6:6 declares, "Not with eyeservice, as menpleasers; but as the servants of Christ, doing the will of God from the heart." We have to be happy with doing the will of God. It is essential to develop an intimate relationship with Him through fasting, prayer, and Bible study. Psalm 40:8 sheds more light on this subject: "I delight to do thy will, O my God: yea, thy law is within my heart."

Following God's will is following His commandments. We do not have the luxury of picking and choosing which of God's commandments to obey. This Christian walk is not like a buffet, where we can choose what we like and leave the rest. Attempting to live like that puts us in spiritual jeopardy. Our souls are precious, and we shouldn't take unnecessary risks with our eternal destination.

John 14:15 says, "If ye love me, keep my commandments." 1 John 5:3 says, "For this is the love of God, that we keep his commandments: and his commandments are not grievous." This means that what the Lord commands us to do is not burdensome or oppressive. The test of our love is walking in obedience to His Word. Jesus said, "Therefore whosoever heareth these sayings of mine, and doeth them, I will liken him unto a wise man, which built his house upon a rock: And the rain descended, and the floods came, and the winds blew, and beat upon that house; and it fell not: for it was founded upon a rock" (Matthew 7:24–25). Practicing obedience is the solid foundation for weathering the storms of life.

The Bible contains many examples of people who walked in obedience to God. It also contains many examples of individuals who did not walk in obedience to His will. Disobedience always brings disastrous results, and obedience brings blessings. Nothing spells this out more plainly than Deuteronomy 28. God was speaking to the Israelites as they were standing on the edge of the Promised Land, about to embark upon a new life. He told them to go in and possess the land. Moses sent twelve spies to check out the place where God was trying to take them. It was just like He said it was—flowing with milk and honey. It was a place that the Lord had preserved for them. All they had to do was obey His command. Of the twelve spies who went on the mission, ten of them returned and sowed seeds of disbelief among the people. They saw the giants in the land and forgot how big their God was.

How often do we fall victim to that same kind of thinking? We allow the enemy to be magnified in our eyes, and fear causes us to disobey the Lord. The Israelites decided to disobey God, and they suffered the consequences—and so will we if we follow the path of disobedience. All of the adults who left Egypt (except Joshua and Caleb) were condemned to die in the wilderness (Numbers 14:22–24) because they failed to follow the directive issued by God. They spent forty years on a journey that should have taken eleven days.

The Lord said to Israel, "Now therefore, if ye will obey my voice indeed, and keep my covenant, then ye shall be a peculiar treasure unto me above all people: for the earth is mine: and ye shall be unto me a kingdom of priests, and an holy nation" (Exodus 19:5–6). He speaks to all of us today—Jew and Gentile alike. We must be willing to obey the commands of God.

Because we are in the flesh, being consistently obedient is sometimes difficult. We have to commit in our hearts to be obedient. It is an intentional act of our will. We decide to obey. Obedience will often take us over rough and rocky terrain. Obstacles of all kinds will present themselves. Hebrews 5:8 says this about our Lord: "Though he were a Son, yet learned he obedience by the things which he suffered." Jesus chose to make the Father's will His own will. The Bible says Jesus "humbled himself, and became obedient unto death, even the death of the cross" (Philippians 2:8). His obedience took Him to the cross to die a horrific death for the sins of the world. He endured the cross for us. Our freedom was His joy (Hebrews 12:2). His struggles were infinitely greater than ours, yet He was victorious.

The journey to obedience begins with surrendering to God. We cannot hold on to our old way of thinking and behaving. Trusting God to be God is what will keep us in the path of obedience. My life was radically changed when I finally said, "Nevertheless." I decided to completely trust God no matter what. Have you ever experienced that "nevertheless moment"? For years, after I was saved, I was held hostage in my own mind by "what ifs." I was constantly being bombarded by all kinds of scenarios that rendered me spiritually weak and incapable of fulfilling my purpose and destiny. I couldn't totally surrender to God because I thought He might take me in a direction that I was not willing to go. "What if" He called on me to experience uncomfortable things? Sadly, the bottom line was I did not trust Him.

But one day it became clear to me that God loved me more than anyone else on the planet did and that He had a plan for my life—yet another light bulb moment. For the first time I *knew* I could trust God with my life; after all, Jesus had given His life for me. I knew that He was not out to destroy me but to bring me closer to Him. When I finally completely surrendered to Him, it was the most liberating experience I had ever had.

I had no doubt that He would always be with me, just like He promised. I had no doubt that He would weather every storm with me and sometimes even stormproof me. He did it for the Hebrew boys. He is the same God yesterday, today, and forever (Hebrews 13:8).

I learned this attitude from Jesus' example as He prayed in the garden of Gethsemane before His arrest and subsequent crucifixion.

The hot breath of death was upon Him, and His struggle was intense. He cried out to the Father to release Him from the impending agony of the cross. Nothing but suffering and shame awaited Him. There was no way around it! He came to die. Painful as it was, our Lord immediately conformed to the will of the Father: "Nevertheless not my will, but thine, be done" (Luke 22:42).

Jesus wanted the Father's will to be done! That's true surrender. There can be no aspect of our lives where He is not welcome and where He is not in control. We tend to compartmentalize our lives, reserving some areas as off limits to the Father. Sometimes we are not conscious of the fact that we are doing so; sometimes we are. We are the temple of God, and He must reign and rule in us at all times. He has to be Lord over our bodies, souls, and spirits. We have been "bought with a price": the shed blood of Jesus Christ (1 Corinthians 6:20).

The Last Word

Living for the Lord is not a tedious task. It is a privilege to know the true and living God and to know that He loves us unconditionally. As we obey Him, we can be certain that blessings will overtake us! Don't be fooled; blessings are not limited to money and possessions. Those things are great to have, but there is something that makes us richer than the world's wealth ever could. Our intimate relationship with the loving God and the knowledge that we will spend eternity in His presence makes us richer than we could ever imagine.

Obey the voice of God. Follow where He leads you. Offer your body as "a living sacrifice, holy, acceptable to God, which is your reasonable service" (Romans 12:1). Be "doers of the Word, and not hearers only" (James 1:22). Jesus has made us an astounding promise: "If a man love me, he will keep my words: and my Father will love him, and we will come unto him, and make our abode with him" (John 14:23). That's communion—God coming to us and abiding with us because of our obedience to His Word! It doesn't get any better than that!

CHAPTER 5

Cherish God's Word

Thy word have I hid in mine heart, that I might not
sin against thee.

—Psalm 119:11

*T*he Bible is the infallible word of God. It is the only
authority for living the Christian life. It is God's
chosen way to make Himself known and to declare
His will. It is the mind of God set forth in the pages of the Holy
Writ. Many great Christian books have been written and published
by powerful and anointed men and women of God, but none can
compare to the book that God wrote centuries ago; it is completely
reliable. The Bible may not teach us everything there is to know
about everything, but it does reveal everything God wants us to
know about Jesus Christ, the way of salvation, and the way of holy
living. When we understand such powerful truths concerning the
Bible, we cannot help but cherish it. We hold it dear; we have great
affection for it. It contains hidden treasures that are unlocked only
by faith (Hebrews 4:2). Not all who read God's Book will benefit

from its wealth. Our intents and motives must be pure. The Bible should be approached reverently and with the intention of coming to know Him more intimately. It should be studied with the intent of learning what pleases Him.

To my regret, I did not fully understand this principle when I was a new believer. I was ignorant to the fact that studying God's Word was necessary for my spiritual growth and development. I allowed the Enemy of my soul to blind me in that area of my Christian walk. It is the Word that helps us to grow in Christ (1 Peter 2:2). Thank God I attended Sunday school every Sunday morning and Bible training class on Sunday evenings. Getting only that much Word into my spiritual system helped sustain me, but it was only by the grace of God that I survived. I strongly encourage believers to get into the Word and stay in the Word—it will stand forever (Isaiah 40:8).

Just because God is the Architect of the Universe and the Giver and Sustainer of all life does not mean He wants to be a mystery to us. He wants us to know Him. That's why He commands us to study. He says to us, "Take my yoke upon you, and learn of me" (Matthew 11:20).

No casual approach to the Word will be adequate because we have an Enemy bent on keeping us from living victorious lives. His evil and wicked plan is to keep us ignorant of God's Word. God said to His people in Hosea 4:6, "My people are destroyed for lack of knowledge." It was available to them, but they rejected it. Whenever we make the unwise decision to skip Bible study or to skip reading our Bibles on a daily basis, we are rejecting knowledge.

The Evil One strategically sets up diversions and uses other tactics to keep us from knowing, delighting in, and meditating upon the Scriptures. God has given us apostles, prophets, evangelists, pastors, and teachers to guide us in our spiritual development. However, this does not relieve us of our responsibility to study for ourselves. Apostle Paul commended the Jews in Berea. He said, "These were more noble than those in Thessalonica in that they received the word with all readiness of mind, and searched the scriptures daily, whether those things were so" (Acts 17:11). They had a passion for the Word of God

As workers in the kingdom of God, we will come into contact with individuals who are seeking an answer, those who need direction for their lives. When we study the Word of God, we can readily direct them to what God says.

Our opinions and philosophies do not matter. What does the Word say? John 17:17 says: "Thy Word is truth." It is the truth of God's Word that sets men free. That fact is clearly stated in John 8:31-32: "Then said Jesus to those Jews which believed on him, If ye continue in my word, then are ye my disciples indeed;

And ye shall know the truth, and the truth shall make you free." The truth of God's Word exposes the lies of the enemy. Experiencing a truth encounter will throw open the doors of bondage and liberate those held captive in every area of their lives. Knowing the truth goes well beyond mentally stockpiling Scriptures. It is not simply an intellectual exercise. It is a heart matter. "For as he thinketh in his heart, so is he" (Proverbs 23:7).

Contend for the Faith

We are living in the communication age. Numerous platforms exist from which false teachers can perpetuate their evil and debilitating doctrine. Satan has launched a vicious attack against the Word of God. He employs any and every method he can to discredit God and the Word of God. Yet every believer is responsible for fiercely contending for the faith. In other words, we are commanded to hold fast to the principles and doctrine embodied in the Bible.

In his epistle to the church, Jude expressed great concern because false teachers had crept in undetected, despite the many warnings given by Jesus, Peter, and Paul. These were ungodly and unprincipled people who used the grace of God as an excuse for sin. They denied the all-sufficiency of God's Word and the authority of the Lord God and our Lord Jesus Christ. It happened then and it is happening now.

We are living in the end times as predicted by Christ and the prophets of old. Satanic deception is on the rise. God's people cannot afford to be "carried about with every wind of doctrine" (Ephesians 4:14). We must be alert and aware of enemy activity within our ranks. As we immerse ourselves in God's Word, its truth will become a reality in our hearts. Grounded and settled in the Word, we will not readily receive any doctrine or teaching that is not of God. As we study the Word and diligently obey its teachings, we will come to recognize the voice of God. Jesus said, "...and the sheep follow him: for they know his voice" (John 10:4).

We cannot afford to be moved or swayed by teaching and preaching that simply "sounds good." Theology, philosophy, traditions, and opinions do not necessarily reflect the heart of God. As we study for ourselves, we will come to the conclusion that the Bible is right! There is no substitute for the truth that emanates from the pages of God's Holy Word. It never needs revising or amending. The Bible is the eternal light that illuminates our paths to heaven. It sets the standards by which all Christian behavior must be measured. It governs the life of believers everywhere. The Word of God is ancient, and yet it remains unchanged. It is settled in heaven forever (Psalm 119:89). As Spirit-filled believers, we must reject all teaching that is not consistent with the Word of God.

God has not changed His mind concerning anything He spoke in His Word. Whatever He said was true then, now, and forever.

The Power of Your Words

I briefly conveyed this idea in a previous chapter. Let me take you back to the wilderness with Jesus for just a moment. The gospel writers Matthew and Luke recorded an interesting incident from the beginning of Jesus' earthly ministry. Jesus was led into the wilderness to be tempted of the Devil. He fasted forty days and forty nights. It was in this state of physical weakness that He encountered the Devil. Notice how He defended Himself against the assaults of the Enemy. He used *the Word*! Jesus didn't just use random Scripture; He used the appropriate passage to fit each occasion. He was THE WORD speaking the Word! Three times Jesus told Satan, "It is written …" and Satan's tricks and schemes were defeated! The Word of God defeats the Enemy every time!

Simply having an intellectual understanding of the Bible is not good enough. The Word of God has to be an integral part of our spiritual makeup. Just knowing what the Bible says does not produce in us the kind of spirit that can withstand the assaults of the enemies of our souls. We must *believe* what the Word says. God's Word is not some magic incantation that just anybody can use to call up the powers of God. Not so! The psalmist said, "Thy word have I hid in mine heart, that I might not sin against thee" (Psalm 119:11). "If we keep God's Word, the Word will keep us" (SM).

Unless you are on a fast, one thing you will do today is eat. Food is important to the physical body. Food brings our physical bodies all the nutrients we need to sustain health and life. We do not have to know exactly how the food we ingest is processed for our bodies to do so; we simply eat it and rely on our bodies to do what needs to be done.

If we don't feed our natural bodies, they become malnourished. We become weak, and our bodies become susceptible to degenerative disorders. Without food to fuel our bodies and to provide the nutrients we need to stay healthy and alert, we would not be able to fight off diseases. We have to have food to survive. *Why?* That's the way God designed it.

On the other hand, it does not matter how healthy we eat, natural food does not benefit the inner man—the spiritual part of each of us. He requires an entirely different diet. The spirit man needs the *Word of God* to survive! The Word of God is spiritual food for Christians!

The Word of God is part of the armor of God that we have been told to put on. According to Paul, the Sword of the Spirit is the Word of God (Ephesians 6:17). Because the Enemy knows the importance of the Sword of the Spirit, he tries to keep us in the dark when it comes to the Word. So often we rely on the other parts of the armor (Ephesians 6:13–17):

> ➢ the helmet of salvation
> ➢ the breastplate of righteousness
> ➢ loins girt about with truth
> ➢ feet shod with the preparation of the gospel of peace
> ➢ the shield of faith

But sometimes our sword is missing in action. The Sword of the Spirit can be used offensively and defensively. Have you ever seen a sword fight on television—or even in person, for that matter? Do the opponents fight with their swords dangling at their sides? Of course they don't! A sword has to be *drawn* in order to use it. It's the same in the spirit; we have to have our swords drawn to be effective! How do we draw the Word of God out to use it? We have to learn to *speak the Word of God*. What do we use to speak? Our *mouths*! Walking around with the Bible in our tote bags, briefcases, or just in our minds is good—but it's not enough! When we speak the Word of God, we are tapping into limitless power! Listen to what Jeremiah said: "The prophet that hath a dream, let him tell a dream; and he that hath my word, let him speak my word faithfully. Is not my word like as a fire? saith the Lord; and like a hammer that breaketh the rock in pieces?" (Jeremiah 23:28–29).

God's Word produces positive results. It breaks down obstacles. It overcomes the negatives. When we speak God's Word and believe it, amazing things will happen. Isaiah 55:10–11 has this to say concerning God's Word: "For as the rain cometh down, and the snow from heaven, and returneth not thither, but watereth the earth, and maketh it bring forth and bud, that it may give seed to the sower, and bread to the eater: So shall my word be that goeth forth out of my mouth: it shall not return unto me void, but it shall accomplish that which I please, and it shall prosper in the thing whereto I sent it."

Do you know what Isaiah is saying? He is saying that God's Word is just as irresistible and effective as the rain and the snow. All the armies in the world cannot stop them. They always accomplish their intended purpose, just as God's Word *never* fails to achieve its aim!

I encourage the people of God to speak (confess) the Word of God over their lives on a daily basis. When we confess something, we are proclaiming it to be true. Confessing God's Word means saying the same thing as God's Word, the Bible, says. Faith to believe that God will do what He says comes by continuously hearing, reading, and meditating on God's Word and storing it up in our hearts (Matthew 12:34–35; Romans 10:17). Any unbelief will render us ineffective at wielding the "sword of the Spirit". No one can have faith *and* unbelief. Confess your unbelief and trust the true and living God to bring you to a place of complete trust and confidence in His Word.

When we speak the Word over adverse situations in our lives, we are not denying what is factual; rather, we are claiming the promises of God and expecting the biblical outcome that the Word professes. Always pay attention to what you are saying and watch your confessions. Do not allow the negative to rule your thoughts and conversations. Choose to believe what God says in His Word.

If you are experiencing challenging or difficult circumstances in your life, find out what the Word has to say about your particular situation. Begin confessing what the Word says over your life. Say it aloud every day. Do not become weary if it seems that nothing is changing; rest assured, when you confess the Word and believe it in your heart, it is accomplishing the job. Things might seem as though they're getting worse, but stay encouraged. Keep saying it until you see results. Even when you are not plagued by troublesome events, continue to declare God's Word. Declare His promises to you (see chapter 12).

We are not helpless in this walk with God. He has given us all that we need to live a victorious life in Christ Jesus. *Speak the Word and speak it often!* There is power in speaking the Word of God. This is what Jesus said in Mark 11:22–23, "And Jesus answering saith unto them, Have faith in God. For verily I say unto you, That whosoever shall say unto this mountain, Be thou removed, and be thou cast into the sea; and shall not doubt in his heart, but shall believe that those things which he saith shall come to pass; he shall have whatsoever he saith."

The following is a daily declaration and I share it with others whenever possible. Get in the habit of agreeing with God every day by saying what He says. Remember, simply declaring the Word of God without obeying the Word will not produce positive results.

Daily Declaration

This is the day the Lord has made. I will rejoice and be glad in it (Psalm 118:24). Today I walk by faith and not by sight (2 Corinthians 5:7). All my steps are ordered by the Lord (Psalm 37:23). No weapon formed against me will prosper; therefore, I do not fear what the enemy will do to me (Isaiah 54:17). The Greater One lives inside of me (1 John 4:4). I am a blood-bought child of God (1 Corinthians 6:20; 1 Corinthians 7:23). All my sins are forgiven and I am free in Christ (John 8:36).

Today I am led by the Spirit of God (Romans 8:14). My mind is renewed and I am in perfect peace (Isaiah 26:3). My heart is free from envy, jealousy, strife, and every negative spirit that comes against it (Proverbs 4:23). All my needs are supplied and I lack for no good thing (Philippians 4:19; Psalm 84:11).

I am strong in the Lord and in the power of His might (Ephesians 6:10). Jesus took all my sicknesses and diseases to the cross (Isaiah 53:4-5; Matthew 8:17) and by His stripes I am healed (1 Peter 2:24).

The favor of God surrounds me like a shield (Psalm 5:12). The angel of the Lord encamps around me to deliver me (Psalm 34:7). My children are blessed and delivered (Psalm 112:1-2; Proverbs 11:21).

I am a winner and more than a conqueror (2 Corinthians 2:14; Romans 8:37). Everything I do will prosper (Psalm 1:3). God hears and answers all my prayers (Mark 11:24; 1 John 5:14-15; 1 John 3:22). Because I live according to the truth of God's Word, I make this declaration today, and I thank God that I have what I say (Mark 11:22-23).

The Last Word

Cherish the Word of God. It is precious, it is true, and it is powerful (Hebrews 4:12). It is the Word of God that builds and fuels our faith. James 1:22 encourages all believers to be doers of the Word and not hearers only.

Remember, when you speak words into the atmosphere, you are sending forth containers. Your words carry negative or positive expressions. Your words can produce life or death. Your words can hurt or heal. Your words can establish peace or breed confusion and discord. Your words can be filled with doubt or they can be filled with faith. In all situations, agree with God. Say what He says. When you cherish the Word of God, He will certainly be well pleased.

CHAPTER 6

Follow the Golden Rule

A false balance is abomination to the Lord: but a just weight is his delight.

—Proverbs 11:1

*I*n my search for biblical principles for pleasing God, I came across Proverbs 11:1. To be honest, it made no sense to me. "False" and "just" were easy enough to grasp, but what did balances and weights have to do with anything? My research revealed that in biblical times, a crooked merchant used two sets of scales—one for buying and the other for selling. This dishonest business practice was used to cheat customers in order to increase profits. Such dishonesty was an abomination to God. In his wisdom, King Solomon uses the analogy of false balances and just weights to teach us how to please the Lord. Believe it or not, how we treat people is important to God. This Scripture shows that the practice of dealing fairly and honestly is something that pleases God. We must not consider this verse to be directed toward business owners exclusively; the message is to all believers.

As Christians, we are in the process of becoming like Christ. No one is born into the kingdom fully matured, exactly resembling God. This is a progressive journey that requires our complete focus on the Lord Jesus Christ. As humans, we tend to be selfish—a character flaw that can hinder our process of being changed into His image. If Christ is not the impetus, the center, and the focus of all we do, pleasing Him is impossible.

A look at the nightly news or a glance at the headlines will reveal that cheating and defrauding are widespread problems. They can be found everywhere, from the corner market to Wall Street. Criminally minded individuals spend an enormous amount of time and energy to devise elaborate plans and schemes to cheat others. The $65 billion investment fraud perpetrated by Bernie Madoff was widely publicized. Many investors were scammed and lost their fortunes because of his greed and selfishness. While he has been brought to justice, that crooked spirit still exists in others.

Dealing fairly, honestly, and lovingly toward one another is God's goal for His children. The book of Exodus tells of the formation of a national group from a collection of slave laborers in Egypt. Jacob and his family went into Egypt to escape famine in Canaan. Having lived four hundred and thirty years in Egypt, the better part spent in bondage to the pharaohs, Moses led them to freedom. Their journey to the Promised Land included a stop at Mount Sinai where Moses received the Ten Commandments.

These commandments came at a time when the Israelites were still gelling as a group. They were to represent God to the world, but hundreds of years in the polytheistic culture of Egypt had no doubt dulled their sensitivity to the one true God. As a tribe of nomads living as one large community, they needed some basic rules of conduct—and a belief in a higher power than Moses who could enforce them.

Of utmost importance was their behavior toward God, which was reflected by the focus of the first four commandments.

Commandments five through ten, found in Exodus 20 and summarized here, dealt with their behavior toward each other:

5. You shall not dishonor your parents.
6. You shall not murder.
7. You shall not commit adultery.
8. You shall not steal.
9. You shall not commit perjury.
10. You shall not covet.

God gave them these commandments because He loved them and wanted the best *for* them and *from* them. How His children conducted themselves was important to Him, especially considering they were about to enter a land whose inhabitants were completely different from them.

Hundreds of years after their exodus from Egypt and their entry into the Promised Land, Jesus enters the scene. God demonstrated the same love at this point in history as He did in the days of Moses, Joshua, and all the elders and kings. In Luke 6, Jesus taught His followers that they were to love their enemies. The Jews hated their Roman oppressors; hearing the command to love them was beyond their comprehension. Do good to them, bless them, and pray for them was the challenge our Lord set before them and before us. He concluded with this powerful statement: "And as ye would that men should do to you, do ye also to them likewise" (Luke 6:31).

Just think about it! If everybody (in their sound mind) treated other people the way they'd want to be treated themselves, the world would be a very different place—a much better place. What would happen to the crime rate? What would happen in families? What would happen in our churches? Jesus was really on to something! We are not responsible for anyone else's actions, only our own. As we live and treat others the way we want to be treated, it will influence others. According to the Bible, the treatment will also come back to us: "Be not deceived; God is not mocked: for whatsoever a man soweth, that shall he also reap" (Galatians 6:7).

If you are born again, you are a child of God. Like any good parent, God wants us to be well-behaved. We belong to Him, and yet He gives us the choice to obey or not obey His commands. We learn the "code of Christian conduct" from the Bible. A code of conduct is a set of rules to guide behavior. In other words, it contains a description of the way one is expected to behave. We have to be committed to those standards and values.

The Last Word

Being born again gives us the freedom and the privilege to live for God and to make right choices. Our spiritual walk is not up to us; we have to allow the Holy Ghost to lead us. Concerning the Holy Ghost, Jesus told His disciples, "Howbeit when he, the Spirit of truth, is come, he will guide you into all truth" (John 16:13). The apostle Paul said in Galatians 5:16, "This I say then, Walk in the Spirit, and ye shall not fulfil the lust of the flesh." The work of the Spirit of God is vital to our existence. As we allow Him full control in our lives, we are led into the way everlasting. Living under the influence of the Spirit guarantees our steps are always pleasing to God. The Spirit knows the mind of God and the will of God. He will never lead us contrary to what God has designed and purposed for His children. Living under the influence of the Spirit guarantees that we will always treat other people, whether saved or unsaved, with the utmost respect, dignity, and love.

CHAPTER 7

Don't Be a Complainer

And when the people complained, it displeased the Lord: and the Lord heard it; and his anger was kindled; and the fire of the Lord burnt among them, and consumed them that were in the uttermost parts of the camp.

—Numbers 11:1

ome years ago the Lord stopped me dead in my tracks with a question. I was talking, but I was not in prayer. My words were not giving God glory. He plainly asked me if I was listening to myself. I began to pay attention—and I did not like what I heard. I was horrified, devastated, embarrassed, sad, and deeply ashamed. I was not cursing or running anybody down, but I was not talking like a daughter who was grateful for all the wonderful blessings bestowed upon me. I sounded like an ingrate! I had become a whiner. The weather always seemed to be my biggest complaint; I was either too hot or too cold! This may sound trivial to some, but it was not trivial to God.

My complaints were an indicator of a more serious problem. Immediately I asked the Lord to forgive me and to help me to always have a thankful heart, in spite of the weather conditions or life's present circumstances. I now try to remind myself often of how great God is and how much He loves me. Things may not always be as we desire, but God is good! Throughout the Bible, we are urged to give thanks to Him and to bless His name.

Complaining was a major problem with the children of Israel from the beginning. The book of Numbers records the tragic story of their unbelief. In the second year after they left Egypt, they found themselves at the foot of Mount Sinai. Under the leadership of Moses, God prepared them to move into their destiny. At last, they were on the final leg of the journey into the Promised Land (Canaan). It was theirs! All they had to do was possess it—but they didn't. The people complained. "And when the people complained, it displeased the Lord" (Numbers 11:1).

Israel's complaining demonstrated a lack of gratitude to the almighty God. Gratitude is a feeling of thankfulness and appreciation for all that is. Grateful people enjoy the simple things in life. They often discover the blessings of God in unexpected and unusual places. These people find pleasure in knowing that God is faithful regardless of what is going on in their lives. They believe what Paul told the church at Thessalonica: "In every thing give thanks: for this is the will of God in Christ Jesus concerning you" (1 Thessalonians 5:18).

Thanksgiving is a holiday celebrated in the United States of America on the fourth Thursday in November. In reality, everyday should be a day of thanksgiving. We can never say thank you enough to our loving God and Father. We can never praise Him enough for all of His marvelous acts of kindness on our behalf. If the Lord had not been on our side, where would we be? Believers and unbelievers alike owe the Lord a debt of gratitude. Time and time again, Scripture reveals God's faithfulness to us.

Amid all the things going on around us—trouble and

tribulations, the threat of violence and fear projected via the news media, and the turmoil that exists within our lives on a daily basis—we can trust our unchanging God.

Genesis declares that He is a God of power. "In the beginning God created the heaven and the earth" (Genesis 1:1).

Hebrews 11:3 substantiates it: "Through faith we understand that the worlds were framed by the word of God, so that things which are seen were not made of things which do appear." That's power!

Then God said to Jeremiah, "Behold, I am the Lord, the God of all flesh: is there any thing too hard for me?" (Jeremiah 32:27).

Lack of trust in God condemned Israel to wandering in the wilderness. All the while they were complaining. They complained about having no food, and God gave them bread from heaven. They complained about having no water, and God gave them water to drink. They wished for the good old days back in Egypt and wanted to return. No trust!

He provided for all their needs but how quickly they forgot.

God does the same thing in our lives—over and over again He shows up, manifests His power in our lives—He heals us, delivers us, sets us free from bondages, opens doors for us, works out all of our problems and no sooner than the next trial comes, we've already forgotten and we fall into that mumbling, grumbling, and complaining state. God is never pleased with complaining.

Numbers 11:1 in its entirety says, "And when the people complained, it displeased the Lord; and the Lord heard it; and his anger was kindled; and the fire of the Lord burnt among them and consumed them that were in the uttermost parts of the camp".

They suffered the terrible consequences of their complaining. The last straw for God was when He ordered Moses to send out twelve spies to search out the land. They were gone forty days on their mission. When they returned, the group brought back a mixed report. They were excited about the richness of the land. It was just as the Lord had said—a land flowing with milk and honey. That meant that it was rich and plentiful. It was the land that God promised to Abraham, Isaac, and Jacob. This bountiful land was theirs!

But they couldn't stop focusing on their fear. They talked about the giants they saw. They talked about the high walls that surrounded the cities. They were viewing things from a human perspective. They had forgotten to put God into the equation. They saw themselves as victims of that land. They saw themselves as grasshoppers with no power to overcome the people that occupied the land.

Of the twelve men that Moses sent, only two brought back a favorable report. They saw the same thing the other ten saw, but they had a different perspective. They were ready to go in and possess the land because they believed God! Those two men said, "let us go up at once and possess it for we are well able to overcome it!" They trusted God to be the same God that had been with them and for them all this time!

But because of the negative report of the majority of the men that went into the land, the people became fearful and rebelled. They refused to take that step of faith to go into the Promised Land.

The people cried and wept all night. The Bible says they murmured against Moses and Aaron and wished that they had died in Egypt or even just die in the wilderness instead of being killed by the inhabitants of the land.

Instead of them going into the land and possessing what was already theirs, they wanted to make a captain to take them back to Egypt. They wanted to return to a land that had been devastated by their God; return to a land that was probably still mourning for their first-born sons; return to a land that they had looted on the eve of their exodus; return by the Red Sea where the Egyptian army had been drowned chasing after them. None of this made any real sense and yet to them it seemed safer than to believe that God would lead them to victory in Canaan.

God had devastated Egypt, parted the Red Sea, fed them with bread from heaven, and led them through the wilderness, yet they still could not trust his power to prevail over a few giants.

God can do miracle after miracle for us. Yet, if we allow the enemy to have his way, we will only see the negative, what is wrong, instead of seeing all that is right. We can always find something to complain about even in the midst of continual miracles.

The children of Israel were to represent God in the world. They were His chosen people. Their actions clearly demonstrated what they thought about God. They doubted His power. They had a low concept of God.

If we want to please God, our concept of God and who He is must be exceptionally high. We have to believe that God is the Creator and Maker of all things. We have to believe that nothing and nobody is greater than God. We have to believe that He has all power and that He can do all things. We have to believe that He is sovereign—He can do what He wants to do, when He wants to, and how He wants to do it. We have to believe that He alone is worthy of praise, glory, and honor. Most of all, we have to know that His plans for us are never for our destruction. God loves us. He demonstrated that when He sent His sinless Son to die on the cross for our sins.

Complaining displeases God. As was previously stated, it is an indicator of a serious spiritual problem that must be addressed.

In Numbers 14:27, the Lord said to Moses and to Aaron. "How long shall I bear with this evil congregation, which murmur against me? I have heard the murmuring of the children of Israel which they murmur against me."

You know what happened to them. God caused every person 20 years old and older to wander in the wilderness until they dropped dead. None of them lived to go into the Promised Land. The only exceptions were Joshua and Caleb, the two spies who brought back the good report.

The enemy wants us to speak and verbalize how bad things are and how afraid we are. He wants us to complain about the terrible time we are having. If we make that mistake, the devil will trap us in our wilderness until we stop complaining, or until we die.

The pressures of life today make it somewhat easy to forget the lessons of the past. Paul warned the Corinthian church to remember the lessons the Israelites learned so they would not make the same mistakes.

1 Corinthians 10:9-11

9 Neither let us tempt Christ, as some of them also tempted, and were destroyed of serpents.

10 Neither murmur ye, as some of them also murmured, and were destroyed of the destroyer.

11 Now all these things happened unto them for examples: and they are written for our admonition, upon whom the ends of the world are come.

It is also a warning to us. It may be somewhat difficult to comprehend, but there is truly nothing too hard or impossible for God. No problem is too complex for Him. Our God is never caught off guard at any time. He is never surprised by any situation that arises. He is never at a loss for what to do. All knowledge resides in Him. Whatever the problem is, rest assured that God can solve it.

We tend to trust God in some areas, but then we find ourselves secretly or unconsciously struggling to fix some things without Him. We often have the need to be in charge or to be in control or to be on top of everything. We find it hard to give that up, to back away and say, "God, I trust you." The fact that God is completely trustworthy can never be stressed enough. He always knows what is best for us, and He acts in accordance. That's why we can and must give thanks to Him and cultivate an attitude of gratitude.

After the death of Aaron, God's chosen people finally stopped wandering and started heading toward the Promised Land. They were finally on target. But that did not mean they would have no obstacles with which to contend. We face the same situation today. There will always be opposition and resistance when we choose to walk in the path laid out by God.

That's what happened with Israel. Some of the regional kings heard about Israel, and they fought against them. The Lord delivered His people, yet they were not satisfied. They began to speak against God and against Moses. Consequently, God sent fiery serpents among them, and they bit the people. Many of them died.

When the people repented, God instructed Moses to make a fiery serpent of brass and put it on a pole. If any man was bitten, all he had to do was look upon the brass serpent and he would live. Now our logical minds might wonder what a fiery serpent of brass on a pole has to do with anything. Sometimes we are so busy trying to analyze God's instructions that we miss our blessing. We don't have to understand God; we just have to obey Him! Just trust Him and be thankful for what He is doing in our lives!

Some years ago I was meditating on the greatness of God when a powerful thought struck me. The God we sing about, the God we pray to, the God we love, is the very same God who formed Adam from the dust of the ground. Unlike the succession of natural leaders, God has always been God! He is not in a line of other gods from the past. Just think, when we talk to Him, we are talking to the same God who spoke to Abraham, Isaac, and Jacob. He is the one who spoke to Moses and all the prophets. He is the God who arrested Saul on the road to Damascus. I don't know about you, but that absolutely blew my mind. He is the Ancient of Days! He may deal differently with us than He did with the people during biblical times, but one thing is certain: He has not changed!

God's characteristics have never changed. His nature remains the same. He is that same loving God that He was in yesteryears. He is the same Holy God. He is the same righteous God. Hebrews 13:8 says, "Jesus Christ the same yesterday, and today, and for ever." Scripture declares His immutability, the fact that He cannot change.

What He says He will do, He will do! When our world seems to be in a constant state of change and things appear to be turned upside down, God is constant. God is consistent.

Because He is faithful, we must be faithful in honoring Him and giving Him thanks. Psalm 92:1 says, "It is a good thing to give thanks unto the Lord, and to sing praises unto thy name, O most High."

So often we take for granted the ordinary things of life. To behold a beautiful sunrise or sunset, to hear the birds chirping merrily in the trees, to taste a favorite meal, to feel the touch of the wind brush cleanly against our faces, to smell the freshness of a new morning—all these things and much more provide us with countless reasons to be thankful. However, the choice is ours. Will we "stop and smell the roses," or will we zip right past all the wonderful things God has allowed us to see and experience without ever bowing to Him with a thankful heart?

Let's take a look at an incident from King David's life. First Chronicles 13 records David's attempt to bring the Ark of God from Kirjath-jearim (out of the house of Abinadab) to the city of David. It was a grand celebration and processional. The Ark of the Covenant had been missing for twenty years from the people, and now it was coming back to its proper place. For those who may not know, the Ark of the Covenant was a small chest built in the time of Moses. It was the dwelling place of God among His people. It symbolized His presence and His power. Specific instructions were given by God as to how to transport the Holy Ark. There was no mention of hauling it on a cart. David's intentions were honorable and right, but his method proved to be very wrong.

Right in the middle of the festivities, tragedy struck. The oxen pulling the cart stumbled, and Uzza put out his hand to keep the Ark of God from falling. Immediately he was struck dead because touching the Ark was expressly prohibited by God. The celebration was officially over. David and all the people went home.

David was angry, disappointed, and afraid, but it was in his heart to bring the Ark of God back to its rightful place. He did not mumble, grumble, or complain. The setback did not still his enthusiasm for bringing the Ark back. After three months, he assembled the people again. This time they were prepared to do it the right way—God's way. This time the mission was accomplished.

There was great joy throughout the land. King David was filled to overflowing with thanksgiving.

You may be in what appears to be an impossible situation right now, but you can still have an attitude of gratitude. As we look back over our lives, we'll discover there are many things for which we can be thankful. God is so awesome and amazing that we never have to worry about running out of things for which to be appreciative. If you're finding it difficult to have a grateful heart, I urge you to sit back and just start thinking about the goodness of the Lord and all He has done on your behalf.

It is beyond our human comprehension what God has done, what He is doing, and what He will do. We just have to sit in awe and give Him thanks. He is a mighty God!

It is a natural response to want to tell other people about something that is wonderful in your life. The desire to share it everywhere you go is ever present. Being thankful should not stop at just a feeling in your heart; it should be expressed to the one you are grateful to, and you should share it with all who will listen. Scripture says, "Give thanks unto the LORD, call upon his name, make known his deeds among the people" (1 Chronicles 16:8).

It won't matter how others perceive you, because it's not about you. King David's wife was appalled by his actions when they brought the Ark of God home. He danced and played before the Lord until he came out of his clothes. His behavior was embarrassing to her, but David was preoccupied with giving genuine thanks and praises to God.

First Chronicles 16:24 instructs us to "declare his glory among the heathen; his marvelous works among all nations." Glory is magnificence, splendor, and beauty. People can see God's glory through us. Our lifestyle must match our praise and thanksgiving. Our hearts must be lifted toward God to receive all that He wants to pour into us. When we are surrendered to Him, we take on His characteristics. All people, saved and unsaved, will see His glory in us.

David gave of himself, his time, and his resources. He didn't just say, "Thank you, Lord," and go on about his merry way to do whatever he pleased. He gave God his all. The Bible is transparent concerning the character flaws of David. It reveals that his performance was not always perfect. But one thing is certain: he had a heart toward God. Scripture declares him "a man after God's own heart" (1 Samuel 13:14, Acts 13:22). There could be no greater commendation.

Our thanksgiving is not complete until we give of our time, our talent, and our resources. God gave us His only begotten Son, Jesus Christ. We must get into the habit of fully expressing our thanks to God. It is only fitting that we give Him all that we have with an attitude of thankfulness.

I'd like to share one more story that reflects what God wants us to know about being thankful. It is found in chapter seventeen in the gospel of Luke. On His way to Jerusalem, Jesus encountered ten men who had leprosy, a dreaded, debilitating disease. Lepers were cast out of social arenas and forced to live in colonies. Because of their condition they did not approach Jesus, but they lifted up their voices in a passionate plea for mercy. He heard them and responded by commanding them to go show themselves to the priest. Immediately they obeyed. (Leviticus 14 contains all the biblical instructions given to Israel concerning the cleansing of the leper.) On their way to see the priest, something miraculous happened—all of them were healed. But only one turned back to give God thanks. Jesus asked the question, "Were there not ten cleansed? but where are the nine?" (Luke 17:17). Only one person was grateful enough to return to give thanks. He received something extra from the Lord: "Thy faith hath made thee whole" (Luke 17:19). That man was made complete in every area of his life.

A complainer always focuses on the negative. Instead of thanking God for what they do have they complain about what they don't have. Instead of focusing on how far they've come in life, and all that God has done for them, they focus on how far they have to go.

You may not be where you want to be right now, but at least

you are not where you once were. If you are in Christ, be grateful. No matter how bad things get, do not murmur and complain. We know how bad things got for Jesus.

"He was oppressed and afflicted, yet he did not open his mouth; he was led like a lamb to the slaughter, and as a sheep before her shearers is silent, so he did not open his mouth" (Isaiah 53:7).

Jesus endured more than any of us can imagine. Yet, he never complained. Imagine the beating, the crown of thorns, the whipping, and the nails. He could have said *this is not fair. No one should be treated like this.* He had feelings and emotions just as we do. Jesus knows what it feels like to be mistreated and rejected. He knows what it feels like to be lied about and falsely accused. Jesus knows what it feels like to have the world come against him. He could have questioned God, but he didn't. In the time of his greatest trial and greatest need, when he was the most tempted to murmur and complain, he did not open His mouth.

Here is what the Lord wants us to see. Just as we can always find something to complain about, we can always find reasons to be grateful. If we are honest and stack it all up to compare, each one of us would say, "Look what the Lord has done!" If you are a complainer, I challenge you to replace complaining with thanksgiving. Circumstantially, you may feel that you have every reason to murmur and complain. But, don't do it. Watch your words and your attitude. Don't complain about anything. Allow the Holy Spirit to direct your thoughts and words. If you find yourself being tempted to complain about something, just start thanking God.

When we choose to have the praises of God in our mouths, instead of complaining and disputing, we create an atmosphere for the very presence of God.

As Christians, we are called to a higher standard of living. As we live out the life of Christ by the power of the Holy Spirit, the world will be able to see the light of God within us. Don't complain, just be thankful and give God the praise! Always have an attitude of gratitude!

The Last Word

Whining, grumbling, and complaining interrupt our praise. It turns the favor of God away from us. This behavior and attitude short-circuits our grateful hearts and impedes our spiritual progress. As we are surrendered to God, the Holy Spirit gently reminds us when our speech is not pleasing to Him. It is our responsibility to bring our mouths in alignment with the Word of God.

What I have discovered and love about God is that He will always help us to obey when we have the desire to do so. No matter what the situation is, complaining is never the appropriate response.

Apostle Paul reminded the church at Philippi, "Do all things without complaining and disputing, that you may become blameless and harmless, children of God without fault in the midst of a crooked and perverse generation, among whom you shine as lights in the world" (Philippians 2:14—15 NKJV).

Make it your practice to be thankful to the Lord and bless His name because He is good, His mercy is everlasting, and His truth endures to all generations (Psalm 100:4—5). My daily prayer is, "Let the words of my mouth, and the meditation of my heart, be acceptable in thy sight, O Lord, my strength, and my redeemer" (Psalm 19:14).

Hebrews puts it this way: "By him therefore let us offer the sacrifice of praise to God continually, that is, the fruit of our lips giving thanks to his name. But to do good and communicate forget not: for with such sacrifices God is well pleased" (Hebrews 13:15-16).

CHAPTER 8

Walk Upright

They that are of a froward heart are abomination to
the Lord: but such as are upright in their way are
his delight.

—Proverbs 11:20

The Christian "walk" refers to our conduct. It is
our lifestyle—how we live on a daily basis. Most
of us can manage to behave ourselves for a couple
of hours on Sunday morning, but the Lord is not interested in a
superficial relationship. Our behavior should be pleasing to the Lord
in church and out of church. Our Christian demeanor should shine
just as much in public places when someone is being obnoxious
toward us as it does on Sunday morning. Our lights must still shine
when someone cuts us off in traffic and even at home, behind closed
doors, when no one else is looking. God always sees us, and He is
ever so pleased when we act like we belong to the Most High God.

I read a story once about a little boy who was homeless and out
on the streets. It was a cold winter night, and the preacher's wife

took him in, fed him, and gave him a warm bed to sleep in. The next morning at breakfast he asked her if she was God. "I'm just one of His children," she replied. He smiled, sat back in his chair, and said, "I knew you had to be kin to Him." That's how we are supposed to live. Those who do not know Him should see Him in us.

When it comes to pleasing God, the Bible is our authority. According to Proverbs 11:20, when we walk upright before our heavenly Father, He is delighted. The *King James Dictionary* defines the word *upright* as honest; just; adhering to rectitude in all social intercourse; not deviating from correct moral principles; as an upright man. For instance, in Job 1, Job is described as an upright man. His ways were pleasing to the Lord, so much so that God even commended him to the Devil. Can you imagine it—God complimenting you to the Devil?

Our Father takes pleasure in seeing His children imitate Him. This imitation should not be just an outward demonstration, but it should spring forth from a heart that is pure and right before God. The word *froward* in the text means perverse, that is, turning from, with aversion or reluctance; not willing to yield or comply with what is required; unyielding; ungovernable; refractory; disobedient (KJV Dictionary). Pleasing God is an attitude of the heart. Your life cannot be right if your heart is not right. If there is one thing the Lord cares about more than anything else, it's your heart—the place where He dwells.

Walking upright is a direct result of our conforming to the image of God as we cooperate with the Holy Spirit. In his letter to the Christians in Rome, Paul warned them not to conform to the ungodly standards and practices of the world. Instead, they were to be transformed (changed in character) by the renewing of their minds (Romans 12:2).

The religious leaders of Jesus' day knew the Law and zealously followed it. They were quick to rebuke anyone who did not adhere to its teachings. They put much time, effort, and energy into obeying the Mosaic Law. To their surprise and utter amazement,

Jesus rebuked them, saying, "Woe unto you, scribes and Pharisees, hypocrites! for ye are like unto whited sepulchres, which indeed appear beautiful outward, but are within full of dead men's bones, and of all uncleanness" (Matthew 23:27). Their hearts were not right before God. They had a form of godliness but they denied the power (2 Timothy 3:5). They fasted often, they prayed loudly and long, and they gave largely, but their hearts were out of order. They had hearts of stone. Humans can only see the outward appearance of other individuals, but the Bible says God looks at the heart (1 Samuel 16:7). If our hearts are not right before Him, all of our religious exercises are mere formalities and detestable in His sight.

Walking upright does not mean that we always act according to the Word of God. Becoming more and more like Christ is a process and sometimes we will miss the mark. There will be times when we won't even come close to the mark—but don't give up! Scripture assures us: "If we confess our sins, he is faithful and just to forgive us our sins, and to cleanse us from all unrighteousness" (1 John 1:9). However, our goal is to always seek to walk according to the will of God.

In all honesty, there are those who profess to be Christians who deliberately sin expecting to cash in on *the grace of God*. They live on the edge—doing just enough (they think) to get by; doing the bare minimum. They depend on the grace of God as a crutch or safety net. This is not the attitude of one who is in right relationship with God, seeking to please Him. The Bible is right; He is a forgiving and merciful God but He expects His children to *walk upright*. Don't listen to the voice of the Enemy. Keep your ears tuned to the Lord as He speaks to you through His Word.

Watching the evening news and reading the daily headlines are quite unsettling experiences for me. There never seems to be a shortage of gruesome stories of murder, mayhem, child abuse or neglect, rape, and violence. Political unrest is felt all over the world. Darkness covers the globe.

Long ago David said, "The Lord is my light" (Psalm 27:1).

Centuries after that proclamation, Jesus came on the scene and said, "I am the light of the world; he that followeth me shall not walk in darkness, but shall have the light of life" (John 8:12).

Jesus went back to heaven, but the light did not leave; it can still be seen in us—His followers. In Matthew 5:14 Jesus proclaims, "Ye are the light of the world. A city that is set on an hill cannot be hid." He instructs his followers to, "Let your light so shine before men, that they may see your good works, and glorify your Father which is in heaven" (Matthew 5:16). When we allow the light of Christ to shine forth from us, others will see the glorious works He has done in us. No one can make the light shine. It simply pours from a spirit in right relationship with God. It cannot be hidden; it cannot be contained! Everyone will see it. A light is a light, regardless of where it is. Light always expels darkness.

Walking upright is about reflecting His image. "But we all, with open face beholding as in a glass the glory of the Lord, are changed into the same image from glory to glory, even as by the Spirit of the Lord" (2 Corinthians 3:18). Scripture reminds us that we have been called out of darkness into the marvelous light that we might be the light of the world. We are Christ's representatives in the world (2 Corinthians 5:20).

We are called to be holy because our Father is holy. We are set apart for His glory. Many professional people and organizations have a code of conduct. Christians also have a code of conduct—it is found in God's Holy Word; it guides our behavior. As Christians, we have a unique situation: dual citizenships. We are citizens of the country in which we live, and we are citizens of the kingdom of God. We are in the world, but we are not of the world. In order to please the Lord, we must commit to His standards and values.

What an honor it is that the Father trusts us with such an awesome responsibility. It is critical that our *walk* with Christ be consistent with our *talk*. No matter where we are or what we are doing, our lifestyles must always be a reflection of the Lord. Our actions and attitudes must always bring glory to God the Father. The world is in desperate need of what we have—the light. Without it, how can they see the way to Him who has called us and appointed us to be the light of the world?

The Spirit of God and the Word of God will empower us to become a reflection of the Lord in our everyday walk. We can be freed from habits, desires, or wrong-thinking patterns that are not pleasing to God. Do not be discouraged if you don't quite resemble Him right now. Just remain surrendered to the Lord. Allow the Holy Spirit to do His work. If you have given your life to Him, you are still His.

1 John 3:2–3 encourages us. "Beloved, now are we the sons of God, and it doth not yet appear what we shall be: but we know that, when he shall appear, we shall be like him; for we shall see him as he is. And every man that hath this hope in him purifieth himself, even as he is pure."

The Last Word

Jesus paid the ultimate price for our freedom—He gave His life. Scripture teaches us that God "hath made him to be sin for us, who knew no sin; that we might be made the righteousness of God in him" (2 Corinthians 5:21). Because of Him, we have the amazing privilege of being in the family of God, living righteous, upright lives that bring glory to God.

Galatians 2:20 declares, I am crucified with Christ: nevertheless I live; yet not I, but Christ liveth in me: and the life which I now live in the flesh I live by the faith of the Son of God, who loved me, and gave himself for me". As we live out the reality of that verse, we are assured that God is pleased.

CHAPTER 9

Pray

The sacrifice of the wicked is an abomination to the
Lord: but the prayer of the upright is his delight.

—Proverbs 15:8

One of the most comforting and exciting things for me is
the knowledge that whenever I initiate a conversation
with my Father, He is always there and never in a hurry.
I never have to worry if He's paying attention or if He's stressed out
about somebody else's situation. He never puts me on hold in order
to have a conversation with someone else. He never says He will
have to get back with me later. It is very humbling to know that the
God of the universe always has time for me. He gives me His full
attention!

In prayer, I am assured that He's not listening just to be polite
or because that's His job; the Word says it is His delight (Proverbs
15:8). The word *delight* means pleasure. It gives the Lord pleasure
when His children come to Him in prayer. He loves to hear from us.

To put in the simplest of terms, prayer is communication with

God. Grant it, there are various kinds of prayers but the fact of the matter is, no matter what kind of prayer it is, whether it's a prayer of thanksgiving or one of petition, we are still communicating with our heavenly Father.

Prayer is one of the foundational practices in the Christian's life. Any Christian who has a weak prayer life will suffer spiritually. There is no way to achieve the kind of depth God desires for us in our Christian life without a strong, consistent prayer life.

Through prayer we develop a love relationship with God. We can talk to Him anytime, anywhere, for as long as we desire. We can pray standing, sitting, kneeling, driving, walking, running—in just about any physical position there is. The physical posture is not as important as the posture of the heart.

The Bible is clear: prayer is not optional for the Christian. Communication with God is essential in the life of every Christian. We can't make the journey without it. Prayer was a priority for Jesus as He lived on this Earth. He was and is God and yet He never stopped communicating with the Father. It must be a priority for us. Prayer must become second nature to us.

1 Thessalonians 5:17 commands that we "pray without ceasing." Praying without ceasing does not mean that we must be praying every waking moment. It means that we have a daily consistent walk with the Lord that is founded upon prayer. Some people begin with a commitment to pray and do well for a while, but within a few weeks their prayer time begins to fade. Even though prayer is a discipline, we should approach it with *more* than a commitment to be disciplined. We should do it because we have a love relationship with God and like all relationships, it will not grow without communication.

God constantly communicates with us through His word, our circumstances, our hearts, and spirit and in prayer. We communicate with God through our responsiveness to Him and through prayer.

A Christian who lives without prayer as a priority, is a Christian who does not understand the power of God. God may use us even when we are lacking spiritually, but without consistent prayer, we are limiting ourselves from God's best. Through prayer we acknowledge our gratitude, dependence and submission to God. When we fail to pray, we are declaring, by our actions, that we don't see our need for God; we are declaring that we are self-sufficient and we take God for granted.

Consistent and effective prayer comes from a heart that delights in time spent with God. Psalms 37:4 teaches us that if we delight ourselves in the Lord, He will give us the desires of our hearts. When we look at prayer as 'doing our duty', we won't pray effectively. When we look at prayer as a time to delight ourselves in God and our desire to spend time with God drives us to pray, then we'll pray consistently and we'll see God move powerfully.

When we pray, our focus should be on the ruler of the universe. The purpose and goal is to enter the throne room of God, to come into intimacy with the Lord. We are talking to our heavenly Father. We are talking to our loving God who has given to us the greatest gift ever known to man: His Son, Jesus Christ. Because of His sacrifice, we are able to go to God personally. No more substitutes; no more animal sacrifices. When Christ died on the cross, the Bible says the veil in the temple was torn in two (Matthew 27:50–51). That signified that Christ's sacrificial death was accepted by God and the way was open for every person to approach God. The *only requirement* is to believe on the Lord Jesus Christ. John 1:12 shares this thought: "But as many as received him, to them gave he power to become the sons of God, even to them that believe on his name."

We can talk to God about the significant things in life and the not so significant things without fear. We have no need to try to conceal anything from God, because we are all an open book to Him. He knows our motivations, our temptations, our faults, our failures, our frailties, our inconsistencies, and everything else about us. He is concerned about everything that concerns us. That's the way Fathers are.

God does not want us to carry burdens, problems, or worries.

He insists that we cast all of our cares upon Him, because He cares for us (1 Peter 5:7). He says to us in Psalm 55:22, "Cast thy burden upon the Lord, and he shall sustain thee: he shall never suffer the righteous to be moved."

There are many other Scripture references that attest to God's willingness to respond to our prayers. It is my hope that you will search for others and store them in your heart and ponder them often.

What Prayer is Not

Prayer is not a canned presentation to God. Prayer is not words we mouth thoughtlessly to God. Jesus warned in Matthew 6:7: "But when ye pray, use not vain repetitions, as the heathen do: for they think that they shall be heard for their much speaking."

Vain repetitions are words that are habitually repeated without thought. Vain repetition is also repeating spiritual sounding words or phrases as though they are some type of magic incantation.

Some people misunderstand the words of Jesus to mean that you cannot make a request more than once. This is not what Jesus is saying. In fact, Jesus teaches just the opposite. Look at Luke 18:

¹And he spake a parable unto them to this end, that men ought always to pray, and not to faint;

²Saying, There was in a city a judge, which feared not God, neither regarded man:

³And there was a widow in that city; and she came unto him, saying, Avenge me of mine adversary.

⁴And he would not for a while: but afterward he said within himself, Though I fear not God, nor regard man;

⁵Yet because this widow troubleth me, I will avenge her, lest by her continual coming she weary me.

⁶And the Lord said, Hear what the unjust judge saith.

⁷And shall not God avenge his own elect, which cry day and night unto him, though he bear long with them?

The point of this parable is to show us that if an unrighteous judge will grant the persistent petitions of a widow he cares nothing about, how much more will God answer His people that He cares for intimately? Jesus used a persistent widow to teach us the benefit of persistent prayer.

When Elijah prayed for rain, he prayed three times before he saw God answer. There is a difference between repeating a phrase and calling it prayer and taking a heart-felt need before God until you get results.

Prayer is not about getting to a certain place, assuming a certain position, and rattling off a bunch of things we want God to do. None of those things are bad or wrong, but that kind of mechanical prayer life can become very tedious. For most people, after a few minutes they run out of things to say, they become frustrated, and then they feel guilty for not having a better prayer life. For that reason, many Christians do not have communion and real fellowship with God. They've made prayer a formal, stiff, lifeless thing, which it was never meant to be. Any time the mechanics of prayer get in the way of loving God, they are a hindrance, not a help.

Consistent prayer will always keep us in tune with God. The Bible shares many characters who lived a life of prayer. One such man was Daniel.

We are first introduced to Daniel in the book of Daniel, chapter one. He is among the children of captivity. Even though they were in a strange land, Daniel and several other children remained faithful to their God.

In chapter 6 of the book of Daniel we see the most dangerous attempt that Satan makes upon our spiritual lives. In this chapter he attempted to outlaw prayer. Specifically he attempted to interrupt and do away with Daniel's private prayer life.

That demonic attempt goes on today. There are mighty foes aligned against us to keep us from prayer. It is our responsibility to maintain a private prayer life.

It was prayer that stood at the heart of Daniel's life in Babylon.

A plot had been laid against him. Its intention was to get him to disrupt his practice of prayer. That was Satan's plot and Satan's motive. The princes and presidents of Babylon were envious of Daniel's position. Their intention was to get rid of Daniel and to take his place. They wanted to remove a rival so they could be promoted to greater positions of power. They were not so concerned about Daniel's personal habits. They just wanted him removed. Satan used their ungodly motives to his advantage.

Daniel's enemies could find no fault or error in him—he had an excellent spirit. He applied his habit of prayer to his workplace and to his life in the midst of the world. Prayer was an essential part of who Daniel was. The secret of Daniel's holy walk in the world was prayer. He was not just a man that prayed but he was a praying man. The devil knew it! If *we* put into practice that same habit of prayer, the devil knows that about us as well.

Let's take a look at the characteristics of Daniel's prayer life. First of all, it was habitual. Daniel "kneeled upon his knees three times a day." He had regular, set times of prayer. His enemies knew about it and they tried to use it against him.

The presidents and the princes convinced the king that, for thirty days, anyone found praying to any god but to the king should be put to death. They knew Daniel's habit of regular prayer.

He kneeled on the floor. He opened his windows toward Jerusalem, the place on earth where all the promises of God were centered. And his prayer was a prayer in which he gave thanks and made supplication before God and came before God to worship God as God. He directed his heart toward God.

The devil hates prayer. His goal and intention is to disrupt our communion with God any way he can. This is the very thing that happened in the Garden of Eden. In the beginning, the first man, Adam and his wife, Eve, had fellowship with God. They communed with God. They talked with God. He gave them authority over everything but there was one stipulation. They were not to eat of the tree of the knowledge of good and evil. They could eat from any other tree in the garden, even the tree of life! So they had only one *wrong* choice to make; and the serpent beguiled Eve into making that one wrong choice. She ate it and then gave the forbidden fruit to her husband. He ate it! The moment they disobeyed God, their fellowship was broken. They lost their sweet communion with God.

This is what the enemy was attempting to do to Daniel. He wanted him to break fellowship with God. When Daniel realized that the decree had been signed by King Darius, he was not in the least intimidated. He demonstrated no fear of what the enemy was attempting to do. He knew His God. The enemy must have been roaring in Daniel's ear, trying to reason with him, trying to talk him out of praying just for a little while, just so he could maintain his position of authority. Isn't that just like the Devil? He'll say to us, "it won't hurt to do it just this one time." One time is all it takes to break fellowship with God. Any act of willful disobedience is an offense to God. How can we draw near to a holy and righteous God when we allow sin to break our communion with Him? The devil knows that when we compromise our beliefs and convictions where God is concerned, he has just won. Daniel didn't fall for it and neither should we.

Daniel 6:10 says: "Now when Daniel knew that the writing was signed, he went into his house; and his windows being open in his chamber toward Jerusalem, he kneeled upon his knees three times a day, and prayed, and gave thanks before his God, as he did aforetime."

The princes and presidents couldn't wait to let King Darius know that the man he had chosen to place in authority over them had disobeyed a royal decree. The king was disturbed and he labored all day trying to help Daniel, to no avail. He was bound by his own royal oath to have Daniel thrown into the den of lions. Even though Darius was a heathen king, he had witnessed Daniel's God in action many times and he believed that God would rescue Daniel. Read what this heathen king said in Daniel 6:16: "Now the king spake and said unto Daniel, Thy God whom thou servest continually, he will deliver thee." The king was convinced that Daniel's God would deliver him.

Daniel 6:17-22 records what happened next.

¹⁷ And a stone was brought, and laid upon the mouth of the den; and the king sealed it with his own signet, and with the signet of his lords; that the purpose might not be changed concerning Daniel.

¹⁸ Then the king went to his palace, and passed the night fasting: neither were instruments of musick brought before him: and his sleep went from him.

¹⁹ Then the king arose very early in the morning, and went in haste unto the den of lions.

²⁰ And when he came to the den, he cried with a lamentable voice unto Daniel: and the king spake and said to Daniel, O Daniel, servant of the living God, is thy God, whom thou servest continually, able to deliver thee from the lions?

²¹ Then said Daniel unto the king, O king, live for ever.

²² My God hath sent his angel, and hath shut the lions' mouths, that they have not hurt me: forasmuch as before him innocency was found in me; and also before thee, O king, have I done no hurt.

Daniel was not hurt! He didn't have a scratch on him! God did not prevent Daniel from being thrown into the lions' den but He prevented him from being destroyed. God sent His angel to shut the lion's mouths so that no harm could come to Daniel.

There are times in our lives when God allows us to be thrown into the lion's den. In other words, sometimes He doesn't prevent us from facing challenging, difficult or dangerous situations. But we are assured that He never lets us go through it alone. He is always with us to deliver us.

In chapter 3 of the book of Daniel, Shadrach, Meshak, and Abednego faced deadly circumstances when they were thrown into the fiery furnace for their faithfulness to God. God didn't keep them from being thrown into that fire but the Bible tells us that He was seen walking in the fire with them. When they came out, they had no hurt and they didn't even smell like smoke. That's the kind of God we serve! They knew the priority of prayer. Just as God watched over them, He will do the same for us.

Daniel 6: 23-28 records the conclusion of the story:

²³ Then was the king exceedingly glad for him, and commanded that they should take Daniel up out of the den. So Daniel was taken up out of the den, and no manner of hurt was found upon him, because he believed in his God.

²⁴ And the king commanded, and they brought those men which had accused Daniel, and they cast them into the den of lions, them, their children, and their wives; and the lions had the mastery of them, and brake all their bones in pieces or ever they came at the bottom of the den.

²⁵ Then king Darius wrote unto all people, nations, and languages, that dwell in all the earth; Peace be multiplied unto you.

²⁶ I make a decree, That in every dominion of my kingdom men tremble and fear before the God of Daniel: for he is the living God, and stedfast for ever, and his kingdom that which shall not be destroyed, and his dominion shall be even unto the end.

²⁷ He delivereth and rescueth, and he worketh signs and wonders in heaven and in earth, who hath delivered Daniel from the power of the lions.

²⁸ So this Daniel prospered in the reign of Darius, and in the reign of Cyrus the Persian.

Daniel prospered because of prayer. He prospered because of his commitment to God and his communion with God. The real danger to Daniel's spiritual life was not in the den of lions. There was no danger there. But the battle was fought in Daniel's room. The battle was fought when Daniel went home that first day after the king's decree against prayer. The battle was fought when the time was come, the set time to open his windows and look to Jerusalem and to kneel in prayer. Circumstances didn't change his habit of prayer. Circumstances confirmed his habit and God showed up!

The Word assures us that God is delighted every time His children come before Him in prayer. Without question, every Christian should pray! It is our privilege and His pleasure. If we expect the Lord to hear and respond to us every time, we must keep the line of communication clear. The Bible mentions several things that can hinder our prayers. I will examine a few of them.

Sin Hinders Prayer

One thing that hinders our communication with God is sin. Sin is any deliberate action, attitude, or thought that goes against God. Sin always separates us from God. It breaks the communication link between us and the Father, blocking our connection to God. If we want to have power in prayer, we have to be ruthless in dealing with our own sins. The Bible clearly says, "If I regard iniquity in my heart, the Lord will not hear me" (Psalms 66:18).

Again we are told, "Behold, the Lord's hand is not shortened, that it cannot save; neither his ear heavy, that it cannot hear: But your iniquities have separated between you and your God, and your sins have hid his face from you, that he will not hear" (Isaiah 59:1–2).

The bottom line is this: "Therefore to him that knoweth to do good, and doeth it not, to him it is sin" (James 4:17). Sin hinders prayer, and it is our responsibility to ensure that the line of communication to the almighty God remains intact. Read what Psalms 139:23–24 declares: "Search me, O God, and know my heart: try me, and know my thoughts: And see if there be any wicked way in me, and lead me in the way everlasting."

When we genuinely seek the Lord in such a manner, He will respond. It is not always a pleasant encounter when He does. Coming face-to-face with your own sins is heartbreaking, but God will not leave you in the trench of despair.

I can recall various occasions when I thought I was doing 100 percent only to realize that I was only doing about 50 percent, probably not that much. What a blow! Though it does not feel good at the time, when we come to grips with reality and realize that God reveals our wrongs and shortcomings for our own good, we are made better when we cooperate with the process. Our connection becomes stronger. We are even more committed. The following passage is taken from the Contemporary English Bible:

> The Lord corrects the people he loves and disciplines those he calls his own.
>
> Be patient when you are being corrected! This is how God treats his children. Don't all parents correct their children? God corrects all of his children, and if he doesn't correct you, then you don't really belong to him. Our earthly fathers correct us, and we still respect them. Isn't it even better to be given true life by letting our spiritual Father correct us?
>
> Our human fathers correct us for a short time, and they do it as they think best. But God corrects us for our own good, because he wants us to be holy, as he is. It is never fun to be corrected. In fact, at the time it is always painful. But if we learn to obey by being corrected, we will do right and live at peace. (Hebrews 12:6–11)

That is all I will say about sin as a hindrance to our prayers, but there is much, much more information on this subject in God's Word.

Idols in the Heart Hinders Prayer

Another thing that hinders our prayer is idols in the heart. That is the reason for John's admonition: "Little children, keep yourselves from idols" (1 John 5:21). Archaeology limits its description of idols to stone statues and objects. The Bible teaches that idols are anything or anyone that takes the place of God in our lives. The first of the Ten Commandments says, "Thou shalt have no other gods before me" (Exodus 20:3).

God alone is entitled to have the supreme place in our hearts. Everything and everyone else must be subordinate to Him. When we understand this, we realize that idolatry is not just ancient history but is alive and flourishing in the twenty-first century!

We make idols of our spouses, our jobs, our homes, our reputations, our achievements, our children, our education—we make idols of a whole range of things. It is not that these things are evil in themselves; rather, it is the importance we attach to them. When we replace God with these things, they become evil. We cannot please Him if He's not the center of our lives. If God is not the single most important person in your life, "Houston, we have a problem."

The great questions we must ask ourselves are these: *Who has first place in my life? Is the Lord glorified in my life?* When the Lord is not center stage in our lives, prayer becomes more of a burden than a fellowship. Prayer ought to bring great pleasure to us each time we approach His throne of grace. Always make Him first!

Neglecting the Poor Hinders Prayer

Proverbs 21:13 says, "Whoso stoppeth his ears at the cry of the poor, he also shall cry himself, but shall not be heard."

Who would have thought that neglecting the poor would have anything to do with our prayer life? Throughout history, the Bible portrays God as champion for the poor. He has always made provision for them. Serving the poor is without question the right thing to do. According to the Bible, it brings material and spiritual reward. "He that hath a bountiful eye shall be blessed; for he giveth of his bread to the poor" (Proverbs 22:9). "He that hath pity upon the poor lendeth unto the Lord; and that which he hath given will he pay him again" (Proverbs 19:17).

Did you get that? Caring for the less fortunate is lending to the Lord. They may not ever be able to return the favor, but God is good for it—He will always repay us. The Bible is explicit: as there are blessings for those who serve the poor, there are consequences for those who oppress them or simply ignore them. When we close our hearts and our hands to those in need, we are cutting off our own supply. When we are in need, God will not hear us. Neglecting the poor will hinder our prayers. Never miss an opportunity to help the poor. Who knows? You may be entertaining angels unawares (Hebrews 13:2).

Unforgiveness Hinders Prayer

Did you know that praying with an unforgiving spirit will hinder your prayers? Think about it. Our prayers are answered on the basis that our sins are forgiven. God cannot deal with us on the basis of forgiveness while we are harboring ill will against those who have wronged us or those that we perceive have wronged us. Anyone who is nursing a grudge against another person has closed the ear of God against his own petition. This is what the Bible says:

"And when ye stand praying, forgive, if ye have ought against any: that your Father also which is in heaven may forgive you your trespasses" (Mark 11:25).

If you recognize there is someone you have ill will against, quickly go to God for help. Ask Him to forgive you, and seek to have a heart always ready to forgive others. You can, by the grace of God!

Peter asked the Lord Jesus how many times he should forgive his brother. Peter surmised that seven times was being quite generous. But Jesus surprised Peter by telling him that he should forgive seventy times seven (Matthew 18:21–22). In other words, there is no set number. He was to forgive every single time.

To forgive means to let it go, let it drop, and no longer hold it against the offender. We cannot thrive spiritually when we do not readily forgive. Letting go of hurt and angry feelings (in some cases, even toward those who are dead), will put us on the right track for an awesome relationship with our Lord. It will help keep the line of communication open and crystal clear.

While on earth, Christ lived a perfect life. He is our example. Nailed to the cross, suspended between heaven and earth, bloodied and humiliated, He forgave all of His executioners. If He could forgive that, we can surely forgive others. It is the Christian thing to do!

Doubt Hinders Prayer

Our prayers are hindered when we allow doubt to creep in. God demands absolute and total belief and trust in His Word. To question God's Word is to call Him a liar. Our prayers should line up with the Word of God. Faith in His Word guarantees answered prayer. Sometimes we go to God and ask Him for things that are positively promised in the Bible, but we do not totally believe and expect them to happen. According to the Word of God, this hinders our prayers. God and His Word can never fail, never change, and never disappoint.

"And Jesus answering saith unto them, Have faith in God. For verily I say unto you, That whosoever shall say unto this mountain, Be thou removed, and be thou cast into the sea; and shall not doubt in his heart, but shall believe that those things which he saith shall come to pass; he shall have whatsoever he saith. Therefore I say unto you, What things soever ye desire, when ye pray, believe that ye receive them, and ye shall have them" Mark 11:22–24).

Faith is the opposite of doubt. It is the key to answered prayers. Jesus said in the Scripture, "Have faith in God." Faith that rests on things that we see or feel or experience will not grow strong or even continue to live. God and God alone should be the object of our faith.

Hebrews 11:1 tells us that faith deals with the unseen things. When we have prayed, we must hold onto God in faith. Faith pleases God. Hebrews 11:6 clearly tells us, "But without faith it is impossible to please Him." Doubt will hinder every prayer, but with faith we can move mountains. Matthew 17:20 explains that nothing shall be impossible to us!

As previously stated, I've listed a few hindrances to prayer. There are others. Please search the Scriptures for more.

If we sense static on the line, it is our duty to seek and search out all possible causes so that we might maintain a vibrant prayer life. Prayer blockers are dangerous and any one of them can hinder communication with the Father.

He loves us and is always there for us. Jesus died to bring us into a personal relationship with our loving God. Being able to communicate with Him without hindrance is critical to our spiritual well-being.

As a new Christian, my prayer life basically consisted of asking God for something and, believe it or not, giving Him instructions on how to carry it out. I knew He was all-powerful and was able to meet my needs. However, in my feeble, immature mind, I did not realize that He is all wise and certainly needed no instructions from me. I learned later on that prayer is more than that. Prayer is an integral part of a personal relationship with the Lord. When you give yourself over to consistent prayer, it develops into a wonderful fellowship with God.

According to Scripture, our prayers should not always be about us. Let us not forget that in prayer, we can intercede for others. In prayer, we can stand in the gap for those who do not know God. We can also pray for believers everywhere. Apostle Paul mentioned several times in the Bible how he prayed for Christians always. We should pray that the will of God be done on the earth as it is in heaven. Through prayer, we can assault the kingdom of darkness and bring to naught the enemies' wicked devices. Through prayer we receive strength, comfort, direction, hope and joy. Through prayer, we can conquer any foe—within or without. Prayer is powerful! Not because of the person praying, but because of the God to whom we pray. The power resides in Him.

Apostle John declares, "And whatsoever we ask, we receive of him, because we keep his commandments, and do those things that are pleasing in his sight" (1 John 3:22).

When we pray according to God's will, we can be assured that we will have positive results. This is what the Scripture says (1 John 5:14–15): "And this is the confidence that we have in him, that, if we ask any thing according to his will, he heareth us: And if we know that he hear us, whatsoever we ask, we know that we have the petitions that we desired of him."

So how do we know that we are praying God's will? When we pray the Word of God, we are praying according to His will. His Word is His will concerning us. When we collect the Word in our hearts with the express purpose of living by it, we are storing up God's will in our spirits. As we pray, the Holy Ghost—who knows the mind of God—will help us in prayer. We do not always know what to pray for, but He does. When He prays to the Father through us, we can always expect the Father to hear and answer us (Romans 8:26-27).

You will be blessed every time you pray when you keep in mind the purpose of prayer. Through prayer, God invites us to come into a loving relationship with Him, to know Him, to walk close to Him, to be like Him, and to partake of His divine nature.

When we pray with this attitude and focus, we cannot help but worship God and praise Him. Prayer is God's idea, part of His plan for His people. God is calling all believers to Himself. He wants us to pray and to seek His face, to walk with Him daily, and to abide in Him.

The Gospels clearly recorded that Jesus prayed. As the Son of God, it was important to Him—what about us? Following Jesus' example should be the priority for us. I learned this the hard way. As a new convert, I naively thought that anybody who professed Christ would be a good role model. Instead of following Christ, I followed them. I conformed to their standard of living. I soon learned that was not the way to please God. We sing that old hymn, "Where He Leads Me I Will Follow." The words of that song must become a reality in our lives. We know that to be true, but often what we *know* and what we *do* are two different things. Imitating the flawed practices of other believers only serves to arrest our spiritual development. Having partaken of His divine nature, we are prompted by the Spirit to walk as He walked. No other way is acceptable to God. Peter says it this way, "For even hereunto were ye called: because Christ also suffered for us, leaving us an example, that ye should follow his steps (I Peter 2:21).

Spending time with God in prayer is critical for every Christian. It is the greatest investment we can ever make. Do not be distracted or deterred by the voice of the enemy or by any of his tactics. He knows the value and the power of prayer and he will do whatever it takes to keep us out of the Presence of God.

One story in particular comes to mind concerning spending time with Jesus and the value that He puts on it. Luke 10:38-42 records the story of two sisters who received Jesus in their home. Though they lived together, they had different priorities. Martha was busy and preoccupied with preparing and serving, while Mary sat at the feet of Jesus, listening to His every word. Martha became agitated and upset with her sister because she was not helping. She wanted Jesus to make her help. Even though it looked as if Mary was doing nothing, Jesus Himself said she had "chosen the good part" (Luke 10:42). She had discovered the necessary thing: true worship and devotion of her heart and full attention to Christ. Spending time with Him was a higher priority than serving. Mary's desire to be in the presence of Jesus and to listen to His words was a far greater gift to Him than Martha's preoccupation with serving.

This brief story told by Luke establishes that spending time with God should be the highest of all priorities for every Christian. Nothing, including service rendered to God, is more important than listening to Him and honoring Him with our hearts. Mary did just that!

It is dangerous when we as Christians become so concerned with doing things *for* the Lord that we neglect to spend time *with* Him.

The moment our works become more important to us than spending time with Him, we have turned our spiritual priorities upside down. Martha's "much serving" was a distraction from the "one thing" that Jesus said was really needed—spending time with Him.

Doing kingdom work and neglecting the King has no spiritual value. As Christians, God expects us to carry out our divine assignments. But we have to keep in mind that no mission can be successfully completed without spending time with the Lord.

I will never forget an interview I saw some years ago of a prominent surgeon who was a Christian. He was asked how he found the time to spend with the Lord. His response should reflect the heart and desire of every born again believer. He said: "I don't *find* the time, I *make* the time."

If we're going to come into possession of that good part that Jesus spoke of, we are going to have to do as Mary did—make time for the Lord! I often say, and I know it to be true, that we make time for the things that we consider important.

Of course, we don't enjoy the same privilege that Mary had; Christ was in her home in the flesh. Though we can't visibly see Him, we can still spend time with Him in prayer, reading the Word of God, and meditating on His Words.

There is nothing more awesome than being in the presence of the Lord. King David said in Psalm 27:4, "One thing have I desired of the Lord, that will I seek after; that I may dwell in the house of the Lord all the days of my life, to behold the beauty of the Lord, and to enquire in his temple."

In Exodus 34, we are told that Moses spent forty days and forty nights on Mount Sinai in the very presence of God. When he came down to talk with the people, they were afraid of him because his face was shining—it absolutely glowed. The interesting thing is that Moses did not even realize it. In Acts 4:13 we are told, "Now when they saw the boldness of Peter and John, and perceived that they were unlearned and ignorant men, they marveled; and they took knowledge of them, that they had been with Jesus."

When we spend time with the Lord, we do not have to announce it; we do not have to advertise it to the world or even to the Devil. Everybody will perceive that we have been with Jesus!

The Last Word

Apostle Paul conveys a powerful message to us through his letter to the Philippian church. He says, "Be careful for nothing; but in every thing by prayer and supplication with thanksgiving let your requests be made known unto God" (Philippians 4:6). The gist of what he is saying urges us not to worry about anything and to pray about everything. That's great advice.

Have you ever wondered what happens to our prayers? What does God do with them? According to Scripture, when our prayers reach the ear of God, whether they are answered in the affirmative or negative, they are never discarded. They are never deleted. God saves our prayers! They emit a pleasant aroma to Him. I was dumbfounded when I came across this passage of Scripture in Revelation 5:8, "And when he had taken the book, the four beasts and four and twenty elders fell down before the Lamb, having every one of them harps, and golden vials full of odours, which are the prayers of saints." He cares so much for our prayers that He stores them in golden vials. Yes, when we are upright before the Lord, He delights in our prayers and He will answer in due time.

No wonder Apostle Paul told the Thessalonian church to: "Pray without ceasing (1 Thessalonians 5:17). He knew the importance of prayer in the life of every Christian.

CHAPTER 10

Don't Get Attached to This World

No man that warreth entangleth himself with the affairs of this life; that he may please him who hath chosen him to be a soldier.

—2 Timothy 2:4

any years ago, this Scripture rescued me—it saved my spiritual life. I was involved in an intense conflict with the enemy. At times, surviving did not seem possible. I lost many skirmishes and the idea of winning at all was quickly fading. My life was out of order, and I was spiritually disoriented. I didn't know what to do or where to turn. I felt like a lost cause! One day as I was reading my Bible, the Holy Spirit "highlighted" these words: "No man that warreth entangleth himself with the affairs of this life; that he may please him who hath chosen him to be a soldier" (2 Timothy 2:4). It was like a neon sign flashing before my eyes! All of a sudden, I recognized what was happening and realized what I needed to do to get back on track.

Every person in the kingdom of God is a soldier, handpicked by God. I had forgotten that I was involved in a war! I had forgotten that the Enemy of my soul does not fight fair and that he will use anything and everything to interrupt my walk with God. I had forgotten that his purpose is "to steal, and to kill, and to destroy" (John 10:10). Praise God for His unfailing Word. It was like a splash of cold water in my face; immediately, it revived me. I was invigorated and able to regain my focus! No wonder the Bible says, "For the word of God is alive and active. Sharper than any double-edged sword, it penetrates even to dividing soul and spirit, joints and marrow; it judges the thoughts and attitudes of the heart" (Hebrews 4:12 NIV). It was God's living Word that redirected my life through the Holy Spirit of God.

Peter pulls no punches about who the real enemy is. He clearly and plainly says it's the Devil (1 Peter 5:8). The presence of the Devil in the world is indeed a reality. He is the master of seduction and deception. He has the ability to transform himself into an angel of light (2 Corinthians 11:14). God has allowed him to have his own dominion of darkness and to war against the kingdom of light. But his rule and reign in this world will ultimately be put down and he will be cast into the lake of fire for eternity.

But in the meantime he continues to wage war against the people of God. Apostle Paul warns us, "For we wrestle not against flesh and blood, but against principalities, against powers, against the rulers of the darkness of this world, against spiritual wickedness in high places" (Ephesians 6:12). We are engaged in a spiritual conflict. We are an elite group of people with God as our commander. He assures us over and over through the Holy Scripture that we are winners. Although we are at war with an unseen enemy, we already have the victory in Christ Jesus. As we contend with the forces of darkness and evil, we are guaranteed that "no weapon that is formed against thee shall prosper" (Isaiah 54:17). We are "more than conquerors through him that loved us" (Romans 8:37).

In addition to confrontations with the enemy, life itself will present many challenges. The key to experiencing victory is our ability to remain focused on the Lord. Our spiritual mindset determines our outcome. Becoming entangled with the things in this world will throw us off every time. Anything that breaks our concentration on God is a distraction.

All of us are familiar with distractions. We live in a busy world that supplies us with endless distractions. We're human, and we tend to be very self-focused. It's easy for us to get lost in ourselves to a point where we lose sight of God. When we become too focused on ourselves, we are no longer focusing on God.

When the Father draws us out of the bondage of sin, He brings us to Himself. Because God is holy, He expects us to be holy (1 Peter 1:16). Scripture encourages us to "Set your affection on things above, not on things on the earth" (Colossians 3:2). Jesus told His disciples, "For where your treasure is, there will your heart be also" (Matthew 6:21). We are warned in 1 John 2:15-17: "Love not the world, neither the things that are in the world. If any man love the world, the love of the Father is not in him. For all that is in the world, the lust of the flesh, and the lust of the eyes, and the pride of life, is not of the Father, but it is of the world. And the world passeth away, and the lust thereof: but he that doeth the will of God abideth for ever."

Speaking of the *world* in this sense refers to everything that is hostile and opposed to God. It is the sphere of darkness where Satan rules. He is called the "god of this world" (2 Corinthians 4:4), "the prince of this world" (John 12:31, 14:30, 16:11), and "the prince of the power of the air" (Ephesians 2:2). We are explicitly told to "come out from among them and be ye separate" (2 Corinthians 6:17). It is not humanly possible to retreat from civilization. That is not the idea. The idea is not to immerse ourselves in the practices of those who are in rebellion against God. We are not to embrace the ungodly principles and belief systems of those who are hostile toward God. Apostle Paul sounds the alarm against such in Romans 12:1-2: "I beseech you therefore, brethren, by the mercies of God, that ye present your bodies a living sacrifice, holy, acceptable unto God, which is your reasonable service. And be not conformed to this world: but be ye transformed by the renewing of your mind, that ye may prove what is that good, and acceptable, and perfect, will of God". Yielding our entire being to God will prevent us from being squeezed into the world's mold. External forces are powerful but they are no match for the power of God within us.

Living a life that pleases God involves a "steadfastness" of mind and spirit. We cannot allow the distractions of life or of the enemy to shake us from our place in God. How effective do you think a soldier would be in the middle of a battle if he was daydreaming about something else? How long would he last on the frontlines if he was distracted? The same principle applies to spiritual warfare. We cannot afford to be distracted with other things.

As we proceed through life, we will encounter numerous opportunities to become involved with things that can potentially grab and hold our attention. Yielding to the temptation to follow our own desires will certainly land us in trouble with God. Some of the things we become involved with may not be wrong or bad in themselves; it is the amount of energy and dedication lent to them that will ensnare us. The bottom line is that if we want to please God, we have to remain focused on Him and His will for our lives. I must reemphasize that this can only be done through the power of the Holy Spirit as we yield ourselves to Him—we cannot rely on sheer will power.

This is the way apostle Paul stated it: "Brethern, I count not myself to have apprehended: but this one thing I do, forgetting those things which are behind, and reaching forth unto those things which are before, I press toward the mark for the prize of the high calling of God in Christ Jesus" (Philippians 3:13–14).

Paul had the focus of a trained athlete. His gaze was upon the goal, and with every ounce of his strength and power he strained toward the goal without fear. He was oblivious to anything and everything going on around him. Nothing was allowed to break his concentration. He knew full well that the prize was at the end.

Athletes today would say that Paul was in *the zone*. Athletes love that magical, sought after state of mind. This state of supreme focus helps athletes in all sports perform at their peak. Being in *the zone* is a state of total involvement in a task without the mental burden, worry, doubt, or fear about results. In this state of concentration, mental distractions become nonexistent. The athlete's mind is riveted to the thoughts and images that help him or her execute with precision.

As Christians, we must have that same singleness of purpose. We have to set our eyes upon God and the prize He has promised to all who finish the race. Paul was a powerful man, mightily used of God. He had impressive credentials, but none of those things distorted his view and interfered with the race that was before him. He told the Philippian church that he was "forgetting those things which are behind" (Philippians 3:13). He was neither taking the time to celebrate victories nor was he stopping to mourn over defeats. He took no time to meditate and muse on the past. Paul was determined to remain focused on the goal that was before him.

All too often we find ourselves living for the here and now, forgetting that there is a "hereafter." We each have been given a responsibility to the King and the kingdom that we cannot neglect.

Jesus told an interesting story in Luke 19. His intent was to make His followers aware that the kingdom of God was not going to "immediately appear" as they thought (Luke 19:11).

As the story goes, a man of noble birth was going to a distant country to be appointed king and then he was going to return. The Bible says he gave his ten servants ten pounds; they each received one pound. He gave it to them and told them to put it to work. In other words, they were to be faithful with what had been given them until the owner returned. They were each to be held accountable for what was given to them individually. The nobleman received the kingdom and returned as he had promised. He called his ten servants in to see what they had done with his money. Please notice, this was not their money—they were not the owners. They were stewards, managers.

As Christians, we own nothing. All that we have, God has made us stewards over it. The story does not tell us about all ten servants, only about three. What we learn from these three is there are those who are faithful with what God has trusted them with—and those who are not.

The first servant gained ten pounds and was commended for his faithfulness. The second servant gained five pounds and, likewise, was commended for his faithfulness. The last servant we are told about gained nothing. In fact, he made no effort to do anything with what was given to him. As a result, the one pound that was initially given to him was taken and given to the one who had gained ten pounds.

Those who are faithful over a little will be faithful with much; those who are not faithful with little will not be faithful with much (Luke 16:10). God wants us to take advantage of every opportunity to use what He has deposited with us for the good of the kingdom. Nothing is ours to do with as we please!

Scripture tells us that our God is faithful. Just as He is faithful to us, He wants us to be faithful to Him and to His call upon our lives. We have been called to invest our lives, talents, time, experience, spiritual gifts, and financial resources in doing business for God! Believers everywhere are called upon to do so until He comes.

When we are careful to carry out the divine mandate upon our lives, God is pleased. This can't be done if we concern ourselves only with the things of this world. When we become overly involved with matters that are not kingdom related, we run the risk of becoming entangled.

That word *entangled* brings to mind things that are tangled, intertwined, or mixed together. It reminds me of getting my fishing line tangled up during a fishing trip. If you've ever done that, you know the painstaking effort it sometimes requires to undo it.

Meanwhile, unless you have multiple lines in the water, your fishing is halted. Even if you do, the distraction of untangling the line can cause you to miss "the big one." The Word encourages us to keep our eyes on the prize: eternal life with God.

As believers and as people of God, we recognize that there is an ongoing struggle for the throne of our hearts. The competition is fierce! Whatever or whoever sits upon the throne of our hearts rules our lives. Whatever or whoever rules our lives controls our destiny.

We have all been called into the kingdom for a specific purpose. God has no throwaway or disposable saints. We are all important to Him, and we all have a place in the body of Christ. If our hearts are taken captive by outside forces, the will of God becomes secondary in our lives. God is not interested in duty without devotion. God has to be the focus and the impetus for all we do. The Lord specified in Exodus 20:3, "Thou shalt have no other gods before me." Jesus said, "Thou shalt love the Lord thy God with all thy heart, and with all thy soul, and with all thy mind" (Matthew 22:37).

Have you ever been guilty of performing a certain task when your heart wasn't in it? Lack of enthusiasm often makes the job difficult to do. Pretty soon, agitation and frustration sets in. Because your heart is not in it, distraction and lack of concentration will derail your progress. This occurrence is common in the natural or physical realm. But the same thing occurs in the spiritual realm. If our love for God and our desire to do His will is not the single most important thing in our lives, we will never be able to please God. We will continue to get caught up in worldly things that have the potential of sabotaging our fellowship and communion with the Father.

Just as idols in the heart hinders our prayers (discussed in chapter 9), they also avert our attention away from on God. We may not be surrounded by pagan civilizations and their many gods today, yet there are some twenty-first-century idols with which we must successfully contend. Most of us look out for the "biggies," such as drugs, pornography, illicit sex, and the like. But what about those other, less obvious things? Sometimes we unintentionally put husbands, wives, children, employers, humanitarian projects, church, attaining a certain status or lifestyle, sports, pleasing people, even our spiritual gifts ahead of our God. None of these things should even be running a close second to God, let alone preempting Him.

No substitutes are allowed! *How do we keep ourselves from idols?* The answer takes us back to the ABCs of Christian living:

- **A**lways put God first
- **B**e a student and doer of the Word
- **C**ommunion with God through prayer, praise, and worship

When we do these things, our hearts will become idol-proof. Nothing will captivate our hearts and steal our affections. Nothing will cause us to abort the mission that God has assigned to us.

The Last Word

We have only one life to live and one God to please. Becoming overwhelmed and overly involved with the things of this world can have a devastating effect upon our walk with God. If your heart's desire is taking you away from God instead of bringing you closer, it's time to stop and evaluate. Experiencing such desires is a sure sign that it's time to reconnect, refocus, and recommit to God!

Indeed, we are soldiers in the army of the Lord. The war in which we are engaged is deadly, and your spiritual life is on the line. This world is not our home. Heaven is our goal. Christ has already won the victory at Calvary. Your responsibility is to remain dedicated and devoted to God.

CHAPTER 11

Walk in Love

And walk in love, as Christ also hath loved us, and
hath given himself for us an offering and a sacrifice
to God for a sweetsmelling savour.

—Ephesians 5:2

*I*f there is one word that can describe the followers of
Christ, that one word is love. The Bible says in 1 John
4:7-8: "Beloved, let us love one another: for love is of
God; and every one that loveth is born of God, and knoweth God.
He that loveth not knoweth not God; for God is love."

Love is evidence of our having been born again. Love is the
Christian's trademark and it distinguishes the people of God from
all others.

I must confess that for many years after I was saved this Scripture
remained a complete mystery to me. In order to please God, I knew
it must be obeyed; yet, I was baffled by the fact that the Father
commanded His children to love Him. Commanded to love? How

can you command your feelings? Unfortunately, I did not know the meaning of the "God kind of love".

It is interesting to note that the Bible does not give a definition for the kind of love God commands. But it does record demonstrations of love which leads us to believe that love is an action word. John 3:16 records: "For God so loved the world that He gave His only begotten Son". Ephesians 5:2 confirms that Christ loved us and He gave His life. Someone coined a phrase that says: "love is not love until you give it away". Christian love—agape—is the highest form of love. This love is kind, caring, compassionate, and giving. Agape is not merely a feeling or an emotion. It is obedience to God as it expresses itself in goodwill to all people. It leads us, as we have opportunity, to promote their well-being and their good.

Our Lord made this point crystal clear when an expert in the Law of Moses asked Him a question to see what he would say. His question was, "What must I do to have eternal life?" (Luke 10:25 CEV) Jesus answered his question with a question.

"What is written in the Scriptures? How do you understand them?" (Luke 10:26 CEV)

In response to Jesus' question, the man answered and said, "The Scriptures say, 'Love the Lord your God with all your heart, soul, strength, and mind.' They also say, 'Love your neighbor as you love yourself.'" (Luke 10:27 CEV)

Jesus commended the man for having the right answer and He told him, "If you do this, you'll have eternal life" (Luke 10:28 CEV). The man knew this but he wasn't doing it. Jesus plainly told him if he did what the Word said, he would inherit eternal life.

It's not enough to know the Word. To memorize it and to be able to quote it is excellent and yet we have to go a step further. The Word of God has to take root in our hearts. It has to become a part of our being. It has to be the authority that governs our spiritual lives. When we live according to the Word, God will be pleased and we can live eternally with Him.

After carefully considering the words of Jesus, we must

understand that we will be judged by two things: whether we love God with all of our being and how well we demonstrate that by loving our neighbor as we love ourselves. This is the reality of Christianity.

Do I really love God with my entire being? Do I love my neighbor as I love myself?

Loving God and loving our neighbor is not optional; it is commanded by God. Our eternal destiny rests in the balance.

That's powerful! Just think, all we have to do is to get the first two commandments down pat and the rest will fall into place. Someone once said, "Love is the curtain rod that everything hangs on." It's absolutely true. When we love God with all of our being, and love our neighbor as we love ourselves, all other commandments are covered. "For all the law is fulfilled in one word, even in this; Thou shalt love thy neighbor as thyself" (Galatians 5:14).

Jesus gave the man instruction concerning eternal life but the man pressed the issue. This expert in the Law asked Jesus, "Who is my neighbor?" Jesus' response to the question is very telling:

³⁰And Jesus answering said, A certain man went down from Jerusalem to Jericho, and fell among thieves, which stripped him of his raiment, and wounded him, and departed, leaving him half dead.

³¹And by chance there came down a certain priest that way: and when he saw him, he passed by on the other side.

³²And likewise a Levite, when he was at the place, came and looked on him, and passed by on the other side.

³³But a certain Samaritan, as he journeyed, came where he was: and when he saw him, he had compassion on him,

³⁴And went to him, and bound up his wounds, pouring in oil and wine, and set him on his own beast, and brought him to an inn, and took care of him.

³⁵And on the morrow when he departed, he took out two pence, and gave them to the host, and said unto him, Take care of him;

and whatsoever thou spendest more, when I come again, I will repay thee.

³⁶Which now of these three, thinkest thou, was neighbour unto him that fell among the thieves?

³⁷And he said, He that shewed mercy on him. Then said Jesus unto him, Go, and do thou likewise.

From this story Jesus told, we glean that our neighbors are not just those of the same race; not just those who live in the same locale; not just those who go to church with us; or even those who look like us. Our neighbor is every person who needs our help, regardless to their race, color, or class distinction. In Matthew 5:46 Jesus says, "If you love those who love you, what reward will you get?" Anybody can do that.

Being a follower of Christ doesn't require any power when its only challenge is to do something that already comes naturally. But when we are supernaturally translated out of the kingdom of darkness into the kingdom of light, we are empowered and equipped to love across all the barriers. The Bible is not just talking about philanthropic acts or deeds. The fact is, there are many generous people who will go out of their way to help those in need but they could care less about God. That road does not lead to eternal life. Our good deeds must be motivated by a genuine desire to please our loving Heavenly Father.

The God kind of love takes us beyond our comfort zones and causes us to embrace our neighbors. We don't have to know their names. We don't have to do a thorough background check on them. They don't have to believe like we believe. If God places them in our path, it is our responsibility to meet their need.

If we love God because He first loved us, we love everybody He loves. God makes no distinctions. All men are of one family by creation. Christ came to demolish every wall of partition; everything that tends to separate men from each other and from God. In Christ there is neither Jew nor Greek, bond nor free. All are brought nigh by His precious blood.

Apostle John sheds even more light on the subject. "If a man say, I love God, and hateth his brother, he is a liar: for he that loveth not his brother whom he hath seen, how can he love God whom he hath not seen? And this commandment have we from him, That he who loveth God love his brother also" (1 John 4:20-21).

God is the source of love. His love has no beginning and it has no end, because God is eternal. God's love has no limits, because He is infinite. God's love is inclusive. No one is left out. As followers of Christ, we are known by our love (John 13:35). When we are born again, God commands that we love Him with all of our being and that we demonstrate our love for Him by loving our neighbor as we love ourselves.

Christian love—agape does not develop naturally—it is supernatural. This kind of love gives not expecting anything in return. There is nothing selfish in it—no demands. Pleasing God is the only motivation! No one can operate in this kind of love unless they have been born again.

According to the Bible, love is the way of every Christian. When love is absent, all of our labor is in vain.

This point is clearly established in 1 Corinthians 13. Apostle Paul asserts that love has to be the ingredient that powers and motivates everything we do. He paints a portrait of what love looks like, how it acts, how it conducts itself. Finally, he tells us that love excels all gifts and the other Christian graces.

Paul reminded the Corinthian believers that the gifts bestowed upon them by the Spirit were good to have, but he pointed to a more excellent way—the way of love.

All of our spiritual gifts, no matter what they are, must be operated in love. It doesn't matter how eloquent of speech we are, how many languages we are fluent in, how well we operate in the prophetic, or how much faith we have, if love is missing the Bible says we are nothing! All of our giving, even the most sacrificial giving, is of no value to God if love is not what compels us to do it.

God's kind of love is directed outward, toward other people. Remember, this love is not natural. It goes against our fleshly tendencies. No one can love as God commands without being empowered by the Holy Spirit.

Everything that God expects us to be and do is done through the power of the Spirit of God. He is the One working on the inside of every born-again believer who surrenders to Him. If we cooperate with the Spirit, love will be manifested. It will be evident and visible in our everyday lives. Our mindset and conduct toward other people will gradually change and conform to that of our God.

Will we come into contact with people who have unlovable and undesirable ways? Of course we will. We may not feel an emotional attachment to them, but the love of God will compel us to promote their well-being. We will have no ill will in our hearts toward them. We want God's best for them. Just remember that the Spirit of God will enable us to love them anyway.

We must never forget that while we were in our most raw and unlovable state, God loved us. Romans 5:8 tells us unequivocally that "God commendeth His love toward us, in that, while we were yet sinners, Christ died for us." We were filthy, deeply entrenched in sin, but the spotless Lamb of God still shed His blood just for us. It was love!

Paul says love is lasting; it will never fail.

Love will remain throughout eternity. God is love. Heaven is a place of love. There we will experience perfect love to God and perfect love to our companions in glory forever.

The God kind of love goes beyond external religiosity. It is a matter of the heart changed by God. It is not simply a feeling or an emotion, but it is a matter of obedience to God. We operate in love on purpose.

No matter how great our service is to mankind, it must be done out of love for God and love for our fellowman. God commands every Christian to love every person, whether they are sinners or saints. Nothing else is acceptable.

Following God's command to love will often move us out of our comfort zones. We sometimes will find ourselves in unchartered waters. Operating in agape is not always comfortable because our flesh does not want to love our enemies. Our flesh does not want to bless them that curse us. Our flesh does not want us to do good to them that hate us. The flesh does not want to pray for those that despitefully use us and persecute us. But when we have been born again and love God, we keep His commandments.

Operating in Christian love involves sacrifice. But keep in mind that the Holy Ghost will empower us to love like God wants us to love. You may not receive accolades and praises of men for your godly efforts; but rest assured that God is taking note, and He is the One we want to please. We want to hear Him say, "Well done." As we allow love to direct our actions and attitudes toward God and our fellowman, we will be bettered in the process and our loving God will be pleased.

It was love that compelled God to send His only begotten Son into this sin-cursed world. It was love that compelled the Son to hang from that wooden cross. He gave Himself a ransom for *all*, to be testified in due time. He took the punishment that was ours so that we could be free. He suffered a brutal and humiliating death— all because of love.

A verse of Scripture in 1 Corinthians 16 captured my attention. It is planted right in the middle of Paul's conclusion of his first letter to the Corinthian church. One might miss it, because Paul is busy telling the Corinthians some personal things while wrapping up his communication with them. It is verse 14. These words are so powerful, and they contain the essence of what this chapter is all about.

Paul says with simplicity as a reminder to them and to us, "Let all that you do be done with love" (NKJV).

The Last Word

Biblically, love is not an emotion but a behavior, a definite lifestyle. It is the commitment to care for others without respect to their response. It is not possible for Christ to abide in our hearts and we not have love for our neighbor. God commands us to love. Galatians 5:14 records: "For all the law is fulfilled in one word, even in this; Thou shalt love thy neighbor as thyself."

As stated earlier, the Bible says that God loved and He gave His Son. Jesus loved and He gave His life. Now we must be committed to loving like God commands.

Make it a habit each day to focus your heart and mind on Him. No matter how busy your day promises to be, center everything around Him.

He could not have made it any plainer! Love must be the motivating factor for everything we do. *Everything* we do must be done in love, or else God is not pleased.

We can all improve our love walk. Make it your mandate to abide in Love. Make it your daily practice to not miss an opportunity to demonstrate love. Love never fails!

As we strive to live the life of Christ, demonstrating this form of love pleases God.

CHAPTER 12

The Benefits
of Pleasing the Master

He brought me forth also into a large place; he
delivered me, because he delighted in me.

—Psalm 18:19

hen we set out to please the Father, when we make
Him our life's quest, we are sure to reap extraordinary
benefits.

My childhood gave me a rocky start as far as Christianity was
concerned, but I have learned that it is not how you start but how
you finish. Over half my life has been spent as a child of God. I can
honestly say that I have never regretted giving my life to Christ. I
admit that my journey with the Lord has been a tedious process;
nevertheless, it has been an amazing journey, one to be cherished.

It has been worth it all to have the King of Kings in my life!
Most days I find myself in absolute awe of this amazing life that He
has given me. What He has done and continues to do in my life

is beyond my wildest imagination. To God be the glory! I readily admit that I have not had perfect performance all these years, but by the grace of God I'm still here. My greatest desire is to please Him.

As children of God, we are the "apple of His eye." That means we are very precious to Him. When the Lord delights in His children, you can expect great and mighty things to happen!

Not only is God good to His children, He is good to all of humanity. The Bible says, "For he maketh his sun to rise on the evil and on the good, and sendeth rain on the just and on the unjust" (Matthew 5:45). From a natural standpoint, even the unjust and unbelievers benefit from the goodness of our God.

If God sends natural blessings upon those who do not acknowledge Him as their God and Savior, you can rest assured that He has wonderful blessings, both natural and spiritual, for those in whom He delights.

The word *delight* means extreme gratification or great pleasure. When we live to please the Lord, it meets with His approval. What we must always keep in mind is we shouldn't seek to please the Lord for what we can get from Him. Even though there are amazing benefits that come with pleasing God, our desire to please Him must not have any selfish motives attached to them. We don't do what we do as a ploy to win God's approval and be in His good graces. We seek to please Him because we love Him with all of our being and we don't want to do anything that will bring displeasure to Him.

The thing that I find so wonderful about this Christian walk is that when we see that we are not living up to the standards of God, when we realize we are not measuring up to what the Bible says, He gives us a chance to get it right. When we recognize that our motives are impure or wrong, we can ask for His forgiveness and then ask Him for the grace to live up to what He desires for us. God never commands us to do anything that He won't give us the grace to do. We just have to trust Him enough to surrender complete control of our lives to Him.

First and Second Samuel record the history of the rise of David, king of Israel. David's passion for God was no secret. Anyone who has read the account of David's life knows he certainly made plenty of mistakes. In spite of his many failures to live a righteous life, God refers to him as "a man after his own heart." In order to understand God's testimony concerning David, one would have to read the account of his life. I won't attempt to review all that Scripture says regarding David, but we will look at him briefly (once more).

Israel's first king was Saul, who did not fully obey the Lord. "The Lord has sought for Himself a man after His own heart, and the Lord has commanded him to be commander over His people, because you [Saul] have not kept what the Lord commanded you" (1 Samuel 13:14 NKJV). So was the beginning of the end for the reign of Saul as king in Israel. In addition to his unlawful offering of the burnt offering (1 Samuel 13:9–13), Saul later disobeyed the direction of God by sparing king Agag of the Amalekites and the best of their sheep, oxen, and lambs (as discussed earlier).

Summarizing the history of Israel in a sermon delivered at Antioch of Pisidia, Paul said of the Lord, "And when He had removed him [Saul], He raised up for them David as king, to whom also He gave testimony and said, 'I have found David, the son of Jesse, a man after My own heart, who will do all My will'" (Acts 13:22 NKJV). No greater compliment can one have from the Lord!

One might argue that God said that about David before all of his unrighteous acts were committed. We must never forget that God knows all things, from eternity to eternity. Nothing about our characters is hidden from Him. He saw David's heart. Remember the words spoken to Samuel when he went to anoint David as king. Samuel wanted to make the selection according to outward appearance. God said, "for man looketh on the outward appearance, but the Lord looketh on the heart" (1 Samuel 16:7).

The Bible does not attempt to conceal or cover up David's sins. They are all very public. In spite of the fact that David was not sinless, he had a sincere desire to please God. He longed for the things of God. The Scriptures continually witness to his love for the Word, his desire to communicate with God, and his wisdom in serving the Lord. We see him time and again doing what is right before the Lord.

David wrote, "When You said, 'Seek My face,' My heart said to You, 'Your face, Lord, I will seek'" (Psalm 27:8 NKJV). Of God's choosing David, another psalmist penned, "He chose David also his servant, and took him from the sheepfolds: From following the ewes great with young he brought him to feed Jacob his people, and Israel his inheritance. So he fed them according to the integrity of his heart; and guided them by the skilfulness of his hands" (Psalm 78:70–72).

David's life was quite a rollercoaster of events—highs and lows, ups and downs. From the time He was introduced on the scene until he went to sleep in the Lord, he encountered many trials and endured much pain. Before he was crowned king, David was a fugitive, hiding from King Saul, narrowly escaping death at times. After he was crowned king over Israel, David dealt with a perpetual enemy: the Philistines. The nation was constantly at war. His personal life was filled with turbulence. His first child with Bathsheba died; his son, Amnon, raped his own sister, Tamar. Another of his sons, Absalom, took revenge by arranging the assassination of Amnon for his despicable act. Absalom attempted to usurp the kingdom from his father, David. Once again, David became a fugitive. Absalom was murdered. Through it all, David never lost his passion for serving and praising the true and living God.

In every situation, God delivered David. In every hard place, God was there! David says it was because God delighted in him. He was restored to his rightful place as king. In his old age, David sat back and pondered over the magnificent handiwork of God in his life. He wanted to do something special for God, so he decided to build Him a house. God rejected the idea because David had shed too much blood as a man of war. The privilege of building God's house went to David's son, Solomon. The Lord God of Israel honored David in a greater way by establishing his throne forever.

Bible history traces our Lord and Savior, Jesus Christ, back through the generations of David. Wondrous things happen when God delights in His people!

I think all of us can attest to the fact that life does not always proceed over smooth territory. When we enter into relationship with God, it does not exempt us from trouble and hardships. Difficult and challenging times present themselves. But as the children of God, we have the distinct privilege of knowing that we are never alone. Our God is always with us. He is everything we need!

Scripture says if we put Him first, if we seek after God and the things of God, the blessings of God will follow (Matthew 6:33). To be *blessed* means to be favored by God. Blessings, therefore, are directly associated with God and come from God. To express a blessing is like bestowing a wish on someone that they will experience the favor of God. In Deuteronomy 28, Moses paints a vivid picture of our blessings "overtaking" us if we obey the commandments of God. When we please God, we cannot stop the blessings. As I said earlier in the chapter, we do not seek to please God for such blessings—but we can always expect God to shower us in ways we could never imagine. "But as it is written, Eye hath not seen, nor ear heard, neither have entered into the heart of man, the things which God hath prepared for them that love him" (1 Corinthians 2:9).

Now and Later

The benefits of pleasing God are not only for the hereafter, but also for the here and now. Too often Christians claim the life after death benefit, not realizing that God wants to prosper us while we live on this earth. God's benefits are both natural and spiritual. There is nothing we can do with natural or material blessings in heaven. They are limited to life on the Earth.

According to the Scripture, after Jesus was baptized in the River Jordan, He was led of the Spirit into the wilderness to be tempted of the Devil for forty days and forty nights. But He came out in power! Immediately following His encounter with the Devil in the wilderness, Jesus made His selection of the men who would work with Him in ministry. They were His constant companions until the day of His arrest.

Simon Peter and his brother Andrew were the first to be called into service by Jesus. They were fishermen by trade, and that's what they were doing when Jesus said to them, "Follow me, and I will make you fishers of men" (Matthew 4:19). They did not hesitate. They asked no questions. They dropped their nets and followed Him.

As the Lord continued His journey along the Sea of Galilee, He spotted two more brothers, James and John. They were also invited to follow Him, and they did. Again, no questions asked. In fact, the written record reveals that they left their father in the boat! Certainly it was all within the divine plan of God. For these men to drop what they were doing to follow a complete stranger, it had to be God. Their hearts were already prepared for their God-ordained mission. I have learned that nothing and no one can frustrate the plan and purpose of God. Whatever He says will come to pass.

Matthew 19:16–22 tells of a rich young man who inquired of Jesus how he could have eternal life. Jesus told him that he should keep the commandments. The young man wanted to know exactly which commandments. The Lord told him not to murder, steal, commit adultery, or bear false witness; honor your father and mother; and love your neighbor as you love yourself.

The man replied that he had kept all those commandments since he was a child. The young man surmised that he was still missing something. Jesus went straight to the heart of the matter: sell your possessions and give the money to the poor. That was a bombshell! The man could never do that! Jesus knew that he was attached to his money. Jesus knew that his heart was set on material things.

When Jesus made the comment that it would be difficult for a rich man to enter the kingdom of God, the disciples were blown away. "Who then can be saved?" they wanted to know. Jesus responded, "With men this is impossible; but with God all things are possible" (Matthew 19:25–26).

Then Peter said to the Lord, "Behold, we have forsaken all, and followed thee; what shall we have therefore?" (Matthew 19: 27). He was basically saying, "Lord, we have left everything we had to follow you! What will we get?"

That's a good question. *What will we get?* What is in store for every believer who has given their lives to Christ? What should we expect from Him when we genuinely seek to please Him? Jesus assured Peter and all the rest that they would be blessed above measure in this life and in the life to come (Matthew 19:28–29). When we surrender our all to the Lord, He is faithful to us in every area of our lives. As we commit ourselves to Him and to His divine plan, we will not lack any good thing. "No good thing will he withhold from them that walk uprightly" (Psalm 84:11).

We Can Claim Every Promise in the Book

Because we seek to please Him, we can claim every one of His promises.

2 Corinthians 1:20 assure us, "For all the promises of God in him are yea, and in him Amen, unto the glory of God by us." He cannot lie! (Hebrews 6:18) Not one of His promises will ever fail!

God has made many promises to us as His followers. God's promises are not some well-kept secret. They are a matter of public record; they are all revealed to us in the Bible—His revealed Word to man. None of His promises have ever been rescinded, and they never will be. None of them have become outdated, and they never will be. None of them will ever expire. These are God's words reaching out into unfilled time, going ahead of us, securing God's will in our lives at a future date.

His promises give us the foundation upon which to stand. His promises also provide security for all who believe and receive them! We are secured by His promises.

We are people of destiny. The Enemy of God and our adversary will attempt to thwart the plans and purposes that God has for us. I have good news and bad news. The bad news is that we are not exempt from life's problems just because we are believers. The good news is that we can claim all the promises that God made to us in His Word.

The Bible says, heaven is His throne and earth is His footstool (Isaiah 66:1). Who or what can set limits and boundaries for God? Nothing can prevent Him from accomplishing His will.

Someone once said, "Promises are made to be broken." This definitely is not an expression that originated in the Scriptures. There has never been a time when God was compelled to break His promise.

Psalm 138:2 says something that is absolutely mind-blowing concerning our God: "For thou hast magnified thy word above all thy name."

How powerful is that? God has willfully elevated His Word above all things, including His name—and we know that His name is awesome! His name is powerful! He honors His Word! What we have to remember is that we can't claim God's promises and neglect the principles of holy living. He wants to be able to count on us to honor Him in all that we say and do. When we do our parts, rest assured, God will always do His part.

One thing is certain: God has provided a solid foundation for His children, one that will never give away. We can always stand on His promises. Are you standing on His promises? Are you clinging to His every word? Do you believe what the Bible says? God is still speaking today. His words are true and faithful. Beloved, I want you to know that His promises *cannot* fail.

Most of the times when God makes a promise, He does not give us a specific time frame within which He plans to honor it. You need to know that while you are waiting on God to fulfill His promises, there is another force at work—the forces of darkness and evil.

The Enemy takes full advantage of this time and goes into overdrive to weaken our faith.

He tries to nibble away at our trust in God. He introduces all kinds of doubts, distractions, and disappointments. But we must be content in the fact that God always knows what is best and His timing is absolutely impeccable; His timing is always perfect!

I declare to you today that regardless of how long you have been waiting for God to make good on His promises, He has an appointed time to fulfill every one of them. The only thing we are called upon to do is to believe God and trust Him to do what He says He will do according to His Word. Isn't it comforting to *know* that we have all of these promises to stand upon as a foundation, as fortification in our times of trouble? It is encouraging to know that these promises will *never* fail. Jesus said in Matthew 24:35, "Heaven and earth shall pass away, but my words shall not pass away."

TAKE THE CHALLENGE

I challenge you to select one promise from the following list for the next twenty-one days. Look up the selected verse or verses. Read the verses before and after the selected verse in order to gain a better understanding.

Throughout the day, meditate on the promise of God. Focus your thoughts deeply. Allow the truth of God's Word to settle into your spirit to the intent that it produces greater faith within you. After you have gone through the entire list, start over or make your own list of promises and do the same thing. You will be amazed, blessed, and benefitted spiritually and naturally as you focus on the promises of God.

1. God promises to direct my paths (Proverbs 3:5-6).
2. God promises rest for my soul (Matthew 11:28-29).
3. God promises victory in every overwhelming circumstance (Romans 8:37).
4. God promises me safety and peace (Proverbs 1:33).
5. God promises me help in time of temptation (1 Corinthians 10:13).

6. God promises to hear and answer my prayers (1 John 5:14-15).

7. God promises He will only work for my good (Romans 8:28).

8. God promises to show Himself strong in my behalf (2 Chronicles 16:9).

9. God promises me eternal life (John 11:25-26).

10. God promises to supply all my needs (Philippians 4:19; Psalms 34:8-10).

11. God promises never to leave me (Hebrews 13:5; Psalms 37:28).

12. God promises to be my present help in trouble (Psalms 46:1-3; Psalms 37:39-40).

13. God promises me peace (John 14:27; John 14:1; 16:33; Philippians 4:6-7)

14. God promises me wisdom (James 1:5).

15. God promises me power through the indwelling of the Holy Spirit (Acts 1:8).

16. God promises to surround me with His favor as a shield (Psalms 5:12).

17. God promises to bless my home (Proverbs 3:33).

18. God promises to strengthen and help me ((Isaiah 41:10).

19. God promises me abundant life (John 10:10).

20. God promises to give me the desires of my heart (Psalms 37:34).

21. God promises to keep His Word (Numbers 23:19; 2 Corinthians 1:20).

The Greatest Benefit

There are other benefits we can claim as children of God. I have listed just a few.

Here is the greatest benefit of all. Listen to these familiar words from John 3:16: "For God so loved the world, that he gave his only begotten Son, that whosoever believeth in him should not perish, but have everlasting life." Yes. Eternal life awaits every person who believes on the Lord Jesus.

Not only will we "put on immortality" but we will be with God the Father, God the Son, and God the Holy Spirit for all eternity. "And God shall wipe away all tears from their eyes; and there shall be no more death, neither sorrow, nor crying, neither shall there be any more pain: for the former things are passed away. And he that sat upon the throne said, Behold, I make all things new. And he said unto me, Write: for these words are true and faithful" (Revelation 21:4-5).

Apostle John was privileged to view that Holy City [New Jerusalem] coming down from God out of heaven (Revelation 21:2). He paints a vivid picture of this "prepared place" that Jesus mentioned. (John 14:2) The beauty and splendor of this magnificent city is beyond our human ability to completely grasp. We can only imagine! Without a doubt, the best is yet to come!

The Last Word

To live with God eternally—that's my ultimate goal. Living in this present world to please Him is my chief aim. If that is your goal, continue seeking to please Him. Let nothing distract you from your goal. Jesus Christ, the Son of God lived His life on this Earth to please His Father. At His baptism, as He came up out of the water, the heavens opened and the Spirit of God descended upon Him. The voice of God came from heaven saying: "This is my beloved Son, in whom I am well pleased" (Matthew 3:17). Divine approval! As the Father delighted in His Son, so will He delight in you as you seek to please Him in every aspect of your life. Living according to the Word of God is *The Way to the Master's Heart!*

CHAPTER 13

Let's Review

an we know that we are pleasing God? That is what this book is all about. We have been exploring what the Bible has to say about pleasing God. The Word of God is our foundation for knowing God's will concerning us. He put it in a book that has withstood the test of time. God's Book is reliable, and it is infallible. Let's briefly review what it has to say about pleasing God.

1. **It all begins with faith.** Our journey with the almighty God must begin with a step of faith: we must be born again. That initial step has to be followed by a continued life of faith in Him. We live by faith!

2. **Watch that flesh!** Scripture clearly warns us that when we are in the flesh, we cannot please God. Leading an unrestrained lifestyle puts us in spiritual jeopardy. Allowing our natural tendencies to overtake us will lead us away from God. Life in the Spirit will subdue the flesh every time.

3. **Celebrate the Lord!** We need to take every opportunity to bless the Lord. He is worthy of our praise. Praise changes the atmosphere. Praise brings His presence! We should never

be so busy serving God that we neglect to praise Him and offer thanks to Him.

4. **Obedience is the key.** Scripture is clear on this point: if we love God, we will keep His commandments. We will not offend Him by being disobedient. The Bible gives us many examples of individuals who disobeyed the Lord. They received punishment for doing so. Be a doer of the Word and not just a hearer.

5. **Don't neglect God's Word.** God wants us to know Him. That's why He commands us to study. The Bible is the most direct way for us to get to know all about Him—who He is and what His will is for our lives. No casual approach to the Word will suffice.

6. **Follow the golden rule.** If every individual treated other people the way he or she wants to be treated, what a wonderful world this would be. Crime would be a thing of the past. It would be a perfect society. However, we cannot expect unbelievers to conduct themselves in that manner—but God does expect us, His children, to do so. If the people of God can firmly grasp this concept found in God's Word, He will definitely be pleased.

7. **Don't be a complainer.** Are you one of those people who whine and complain about everything? Stop and listen to yourself sometimes. What's coming out of your mouth? Ask the Holy Spirit to nudge you every time you start to complain, and then adjust your conversation accordingly. God will be pleased.

8. **Walk upright.** When we say *walk*, we are talking about our conduct; it is our lifestyle—how we live on a daily basis. When we accept Christ as our Savior, we are born into a royal family: the family of God. As God's children, we are an extension of Him. We represent Him. No matter where we are or what we are doing, our lifestyles must always be

a reflection of the Lord. God takes pleasure in seeing His children act like Him.

9. **Pray**! Prayer is our only means of communicating with God. Prayer should be the most natural thing in the world for believers. It is talking to the Father and getting to know Him. It is the process of developing a love relationship with Him. We can talk to Him anytime, anywhere, for as long as we desire. God delights in His children coming to Him in prayer.

10. **Don't get attached to this world**. That's sound advice for every believer. We must all be aware that in addition to confrontations with the Enemy of our souls, life will present many challenges. The key to experiencing the victory over these issues is our ability to remain focused on the Lord. Our spiritual mindset determines our outcome. Becoming entangled with the things in this world will throw us off every time. When we grasp the teaching of Scripture that we are in the world but not of the world (John 15:19), we position ourselves to please Him who has called us.

11. **Walk in love.** When we are born again, God commands that we love Him with all of our being and that we demonstrate our love for Him by loving our neighbor as we love ourselves. This love is not to be mistaken for feelings or emotions. It is the highest form of love—it is agape. It is the necessary element that must be factored into everything we do as Christians. According to the Bible, love is the way of every Christian. When love is absent, all of our labor is in vain.

12. **The benefits of pleasing the master.** When the Lord delights in His children, you can expect great and mighty things from Him! The benefits of pleasing God are not only for the hereafter, but also for the here and now. God wants to prosper us in every way while we live on this Earth. God's benefits are both natural and spiritual.

The Very Last Word

Living for the Lord is indeed an exciting journey. Seeking to please Him by following His teachings and commands continues to be my daily quest; I trust that it is yours as well. Be blessed in your quest!

Printed in the United States
By Bookmasters